JAMESTOWN
ENGLISH, YES!
INTERMEDIATE, LEVE

D1305905

Learning English Through Literature

BURTON GOODMAN

JAMESTOWN PUBLISHERS

a division of NTC/CONTEMPORARY PUBLISHING GROUP
Lincolnwood, Illinois USA

Library of Congress Cataloging-in-Publication Data
Goodman, Burton.
    English, yes!: Intermediate level two: learning English through
literature/Burton Goodman.
        p. cm.
    ISBN 0-89061-793-7 (alk. paper)
    1. English language–Textbooks for foreign speakers.
2. Literature–Collections. 3. Readers. I. Title.
PE1128.G6184   1996
428.6'4–dc20
                                                    95–39825
                                                    CIP

Cover Image: Boden/Ledingham/masterfile

ISBN: 0-89061-793-7

Acknowledgments are on page v, which is to be considered an extension of this copyright page.

Published by Jamestown Publishers,
a division of NTC/Contemporary Publishing Group, Inc.,
4255 West Touhy Avenue,
Lincolnwood (Chicago), Illinois 60712-1975 U.S.A.
© 1996 Burton Goodman

7 8 9 10 11 12 13 14 15 C U S C U S 0 1 9 8 7 6 5 4 3 2 1

CONTENTS

ACKNOWLEDGMENTS

Acknowledgment is gratefully made to the following publishers, authors, and agents for permission to reprint these works. Adaptations and/or abridgments are by Burton Goodman.

"Shoes for Hector." From *El Bronx Remembered, A Novella and Stories.* Copyright © 1975 by Nicholasa Mohr. Selection reprinted by permission of HarperCollins Publishers.

"Kaddo's Wall." From *The Cow-Tail Switch and Other West African Stories* by Harold Courlander and George Herzog. Copyright © 1947, 1975 by Harold Courlander. Reprinted by permission of Henry Holt and Company, Inc.

"The Comeback." From *Fly Like an Eagle and Other Stories* by Elizabeth Van Steenwyk. Copyright © 1978 by Elizabeth Van Steenwyk. Reprinted by permission of Walker and Company, 435 Hudson Street, New York, New York 10014, 1-800-289-2553. All rights reserved.

JAMESTOWN PUBLISHERS

ENGLISH, YES!

INTERMEDIATE, LEVEL TWO

THE BOY WHO DREW CATS

by Lafcadio Hearn

THE BOY WHO DREW CATS

by Lafcadio Hearn

PART 1

This is a ghost story. It is probably different from any ghost story that you have ever read.

A long time ago, in a small village in Japan, there lived a poor farmer and his wife. They were good, hardworking people. But since they had several children and money was **scarce**, they found it difficult to feed them all.

5   As soon as the children could walk, they helped their parents. When the children got older, they worked on the farm. The youngest child, however, a little boy, did not seem to be fit for hard work. This child was very clever. He was more clever than any of his brothers and sisters. But he was so weak and small that people said he would

10   never grow up to be very big. His parents thought that it might be better for him to become a priest than to be a farmer.

One day they took the boy to the temple in the village and spoke to the priest who lived in the temple. They asked the priest if the little boy could be his assistant. They asked the priest if he could

15   educate their son and teach the boy how to be a priest.

The old man thought about this for a while. Then he spoke kindly to the boy and asked him some questions that were very hard to answer. The boy answered each question very well. The priest immediately realized that the child was very intelligent, and he

20   agreed to educate the boy and to let him be his assistant.

The boy learned quickly. He listened carefully to the priest and understood everything that the priest taught him. The boy usually was **obedient** and did what the priest said. But the boy had one fault. He loved to draw cats.

25   Whenever he was alone he drew cats. He drew them in the margins of the priest's books. He drew them on the screens in the temple. He drew them on the walls and on the pillars. He drew them wherever he could.

The priest told him **over and over** that it was not right to draw
cats all over the place. But the boy did not stop drawing cats. He
drew them because he could not stop himself. Something deep
inside him made him draw cats. For this reason he was not quite fit
to be an assistant at the temple. A good assistant should spend his
spare time studying and reading books.

One day the boy drew some beautiful pictures of cats on a large
screen in the temple. The priest looked at the pictures and spoke
severely to the boy. "My boy," he said, "you must leave this temple
at once. It is not possible for you to become a good priest. But
perhaps you could be a great artist. Now let me give you one last
piece of advice. Be sure never to forget it. *Stay away from large
places at night. Stay in small places!*"

The boy did not know what the priest meant by saying, "Stay
away from large places. Stay in small places." The boy thought about
this while he tied up his little bundle of clothes and prepared to
leave. But the boy could not understand the meaning of those
words. And since he was embarrassed to discuss this with the
priest, the boy said good-bye and left the temple.

The boy departed very sorrowfully. He wondered what to do. He
knew that if he went straight home, his father would punish him for
disobeying the priest. Therefore, the boy was afraid to go home.
Suddenly he remembered that in the next village, twelve miles away,
there was a very large temple. He had heard that there were several
priests at that temple. The boy **made up his mind** to go to the
village and speak to the priests and ask them if he could be
their assistant.

Put an *x* in the box next to the correct answer.

Reading Comprehension

1. The farmer and his wife were
- ☐ **a.** very lazy.
- ☐ **b.** very rich.
- ☒ **c.** hardworking people.

2. As soon as the children could work, they
- ☐ **a.** asked for food.
- ☒ **b.** helped their parents.
- ☐ **c.** began to play.

3. The youngest child was very
- ☒ **a.** clever.
- ☐ **b.** strong.
- ☐ **c.** foolish.

4. The boy loved to spend his time
- ☐ **a.** studying.
- ☐ **b.** reading.
- ☒ **c.** drawing cats.

5. The priest told the boy to
- ☐ **a.** become a farmer.
- ☐ **b.** study drawing.
- ☒ **c.** stay away from large places at night.

6. How far away was the next village?
- ☐ **a.** about a mile
- ☒ **b.** twelve miles
- ☐ **c.** twenty miles

Vocabulary

7. It was hard for them to feed their children because money was scarce. The word *scarce* means
- ☐ **a.** easy to get.
- ☒ **b.** hard to get.
- ☐ **c.** worth nothing.

8. The boy was usually obedient and did what the priest said. A person who is *obedient*
- ☒ **a.** obeys, or follows orders.
- ☐ **b.** is always happy.
- ☐ **c.** fights with everyone.

Idioms

9. The priest told the boy over and over that it was wrong to draw cats. The idiom *over and over* means
- ☐ **a.** high above.
- ☐ **b.** very sadly.
- ☒ **c.** often.

10. The boy made up his mind to go to a nearby village. When you *make up your mind*, you
- ☒ **a.** decide.
- ☐ **b.** worry.
- ☐ **c.** shout.

How many questions did you answer correctly? Circle your score. Then fill in your score on the Score Chart on page 184.

Number Correct	1	2	3	4	5	6	7	8	9	10
Score	10	20	30	40	50	60	70	80	90	100

Exercise A

Understanding the story. Answer each question by writing a complete sentence. Begin each sentence with a capital letter, and end each sentence with a period. You may use the line numbers in parentheses to help you. The first sentence has been done for you.

1. What did the children do as soon as they could walk? (5)

   They helped their parents.

2. What did the children do when they got older? (6)

   they worked on the Farm.

3. How clever was the youngest child? (8)

   He was more clever than Any of His Brother.

4. What did the boy's parents want the boy to become? (10)

   To become a priest than to be A Farmer.

5. What did the priest ask the boy? (17)

   Questions that were very hard to answer.

6. How did the boy answer each question? (18)

   very well.

7. What did the boy love to do? (24)

   To draw cats.

8. How should a good assistant spend his spare time? (33)

   studying and Reading Books

9. Where was the next village? (51)

   twelve milles away

10. What was the boy going to ask the priests? (54)

    If he could be their Assistant

Exercise B
Part A
Putting events in order. Put the events in the order in which they occurred. You may look back at the story. The first one has been done for you.

1. _d_
2. _b_
3. _a_
4. _c_
5. _e_
6. _g_
7. _f_

a. The priest asked the boy some hard questions.

b. They asked the priest to teach the boy how to be a priest.

c. The boy answered each question very well.

d. A farmer and his wife took their son to a priest.

e. The priest told the boy not to draw cats.

f. The boy decided to go to the temple in the next village.

g. The priest told the boy to leave the temple.

Part B
Now list the correct order of the events on the lines below. The first one has been done for you.

1. _A farmer and his wife took their son to a priest._

2. they asked the Priest to teach the boy How to be A Priest

3. the Priest asked the boy some Hard question

4. the boy answered each question very well.

5. the Priest told the boy not to draw cats.

6. the Priest told the boy to leave the temple.

7. the boy decided to go to the temple in the Next village.

Exercise C

Adding vocabulary. On the left are 10 words from the story. Complete each sentence by adding the correct word. The first one has been done for you.

✓ **punish**

bundle(bulto)

✓ **clever**

< **departed**

✓ **educate** *

✓ **disobeying**

✓ **pillars**

✓ **assistant**

✓ **severely**

✓ **margins**(margen)

apenas → scarce

1. The boy was very smart. He was more
_____clever_____ than any of his brothers or sisters.

2. They asked the priest to teach their son. The priest
agreed to __educate__ the boy.

3. The boy drew cats all over the temple. He drew them on
the ___Pillars___ that held up the building.

4. The boy helped the priest. The boy was the priest's
__assistant__.

5. He drew cats on the edges of the pages. He drew them
in the __margins__ of the books.

6. The priest was angry with the boy. The priest spoke to
him __severely__.

7. The boy gathered his clothing. Then he tied up his
__bundle__ of clothes and got ready to leave.

8. The boy did not listen to the priest. Therefore, the
boy was sent away for __disobeying__ him.

9. The boy was afraid to go home. He knew that his father
would __punish__ him.

10. The boy left the temple. He was very sad when
he __Departed__.

Exercise D

Using verbs correctly. Fill in each blank using the **past tense** of the regular (1–10) and irregular (11–20) verb in parentheses. The first one has been done for you.

1. A farmer and his wife _____*lived*_____ in a small village. (live)

2. The children ___helped___ their parents. (help)

3. They ___worked___ on the farm. (work)

4. They ___asked___ the priest to teach their son. (ask)

5. The boy ___answered___ the questions very well. (answer)

6. He ___Learned___ very quickly. (learn)

7. The boy ___Listened___ carefully to the priest. (listen)

8. He ___loved___ to draw cats. (love)

9. The priest ___Looked___ at the pictures. (look)

10. The boy ___Wondered___ what to do. (wonder)

11. They ___Found___ it difficult to feed all their children. (find)

12. His parents ___thought___ he should be a priest. (think)

13. They ___took___ the boy to a priest in the village. (take)

14. The old man ___spoke___ kindly to the boy. (speak)

15. The boy ___drew___ cats whenever he could. (draw)

16. The priest ___told___ the boy to stop drawing cats. (tell)

17. Something ___made___ him draw cats. (make)

18. He ___said___ good-bye to the priest. (say)

19. Then the boy ___left___ the temple. (leave)

20. He knew that if he ___went___ home, his father would be angry. (go)

Exercise E

Part A

Word study. Fill in the blanks by writing the correct word. Use each word once.

draw   draws   drew   drawing   drawings

1. The boy loved to _____ draw _____ cats.

2. The boy _____ drew _____ pictures of cats whenever he could.

3. The boy's _____ drawings _____ were very good.

4. A boy who _____ draw _____ cats all the time should be an artist.

5. The boy was _____ drawing _____ a picture of a cat when the priest came in.

Part B

Fill in each blank by adding the correct word. Use each word once.

punish   punishes   punished   punishing   punishment

1. The boy was afraid that his father would _____ punish _____ him.

2. His father had never _____ punished _____ him before.

3. The boy wondered what his _____ punishment _____ would be.

4. The priest did not think he was _____ punishing _____ the boy by asking him to leave.

5. His mother _____ punishs . _____ him whenever he doesn't do his homework.

Exercise F

Vocabulary review. Write a complete sentence for each word or group of words.

1. clever _the boy was clever with the Priest._

2. departed _He was very sand Whe He Departed to other village_

3. educate _the Priest educate the boy._

4. disobeying _the boy was disobeying when he draw cats on the wall_

5. punish _the boy was afraid to go home when He Knew that his father would Punish Him_

6. assistant _the boy help the priest, the boy was the Priest's Assistant_

7. scarce _whe we don't work the money scarce and we have to Find How to eat._

8. obedient _the word of God is teaching me to be obedient In His Word._

9. over and over _the boy was drawing cat over and over on the wall and the priest got mad._

10. made up his (or her) mind _I made up my mind to go See my case manager to Know when is my Release day._

SHARING WITH OTHERS

Everyone can learn by sharing ideas. Meet with your partner or group to discuss these questions. Write your answer to one of the questions.

◆ The priest asked the boy some hard questions. The boy answered them very well. What do you think the priest might have asked the boy? Make up three questions.

◆ Make up one question the priest might have asked the boy. Write the boy's answer.

1- ARe you going to obey me in the CHURe.

2- ARe You will to Pay the Price to become A Priestee.

3- You Have to get up ot 3:00 oclock everymorning to priest.

answeR:

11 - Absolwitely

2- Yes, Sir

3- NO, Problems.

PART 2

Yes, the boy decided to go to the neighboring village. He decided to speak to the priests at the temple and ask them if he could be their assistant.

That temple, however, was closed. But the boy did not know this. The temple was closed because a goblin[1] had scared away the priests and had taken **possession** of the temple. Later, some brave **warriors** went to the temple at night to kill the goblin. Those warriors were never seen alive again.

The boy had never heard this story about the temple, so he walked all the way to the village. He hoped that the priests there would treat him kindly.

When he got to the village it was dark, and all the people were asleep. But he saw the temple. It was on top of a large hill at the end of the biggest street in the village. The boy saw light coming from inside the temple.

According to the story, the goblin used to keep on that light to tempt lonely strangers who were looking for shelter. The boy **looked forward to** meeting the priests, so he went up to the temple and listened at the door. There was no sound inside. He knocked on the door and waited, but nobody answered. He knocked again. Still nobody answered. At last he pushed the door gently. It slowly swung open. The boy was pleased that the door had not been locked. He went in and looked around. He saw the light from a lamp, but there was no priest in the temple.

He thought that a priest would arrive very soon, so he sat down and waited. Then he noticed that everything in the temple was covered with dust and that there were spider webs everywhere.

1. *goblin*: a kind of ghost that can change its appearance.

He thought to himself, "I am sure that the priests could use an assistant to keep this place clean." He wondered why they had allowed everything to get so dusty. What pleased him very much, however, were some big white screens. "These are very good to draw cats on," he said. Then, even though he was very tired, he began to draw cats.

He drew many cats all over the screens. Then he began to feel very sleepy. He was just about to lie down and go to sleep when he suddenly remembered what the priest had told him: "*Stay away from large places at night. Stay in small places!*"

The temple was very large. He was all alone. As he thought about these words, he began to feel frightened. He decided to look for a *small* place in which to sleep. He found a little closet with a sliding door. He stepped into the closet and slid the door shut. Then he curled up and fell fast asleep.

In the middle of the night, he was awakened by a horrible noise. It was the sound of fighting and screaming. The noise was so terrible that he was afraid to open the door even just a bit to peek out. He stayed very still and waited.

The light in the temple went out, but the horrible sounds continued. They became louder and more frightening. The whole temple shook. Then, after a very long time, there was silence. Still, the boy was afraid to move. He did not move until the morning sun shone into the room and the light of the sun touched the closet.

Then very slowly and **cautiously** the boy got out of his hiding place and looked around. He saw that the floor of the temple was covered with blood. In the middle of the floor, he saw something lying dead. It was a huge rat—a goblin rat! It was bigger than a cow!

But who or what could have killed that huge goblin rat? There was no person or creature in the room.

The boy continued to look around. Then he saw the drawings of the cats that he had painted the night before. He saw that their mouths were red and wet with blood. Then he realized that the goblin had been killed by the cats that he had drawn. The boy understood, for the first time, the power of his drawings and why the priest had said to him, "Stay away from large places at night. Stay in small places!"

Later the boy became a famous artist. Today his paintings of cats can be seen everywhere in Japan.

YOU CAN ANSWER THESE QUESTIONS

Put an *x* in the box next to the correct answer.

Reading Comprehension

1. The temple was closed because a goblin had
- ❑ **a.** bought it.
- ❑ **b.** put a lock on the door.
- ☒ **c.** scared away the priests.

2. Where was the temple?
- ☒ **a.** on top of a large hill
- ❑ **b.** at the end of a small road
- ❑ **c.** in the middle of a garden

3. Everything in the temple was covered with
- ☒ **a.** dust.
- ❑ **b.** mud.
- ❑ **c.** sand.

4. Where did the boy sleep?
- ❑ **a.** on the floor
- ☒ **b.** in a little closet
- ❑ **c.** on a bed

5. During the night, the boy was awakened by
- ❑ **a.** loud music.
- ❑ **b.** a dog barking.
- ☒ **c.** the sound of fighting and screaming.

6. The goblin rat was killed by
- ☒ **a.** the cats the boy had drawn.
- ❑ **b.** some priests.
- ❑ **c.** people from the village.

Vocabulary

7. The goblin took possession of the temple. When you take *possession* of something, you
- ☒ **a.** break it.
- ❑ **b.** sell it.
- ❑ **c.** own it.

8. The warriors went to the temple to kill the goblin. A *warrior* is someone who
- ☒ **a.** fights.
- ❑ **b.** writes.
- ❑ **c.** sings.

9. The boy got out of his hiding place slowly and cautiously. The word *cautiously* means
- ❑ **a.** very angrily.
- ☒ **b.** very carefully.
- ❑ **c.** very quickly.

Idioms

10. The boy looked forward to meeting the priests. When you *look forward to* doing something, you
- ❑ **a.** want to do it very much.
- ❑ **b.** are afraid.
- ☒ **c.** do not know what to do.

How many questions did you answer correctly? Circle your score. Then fill in your score on the Score Chart on page 184.

Number Correct	1	2	3	4	5	6	7	8	9	10
Score	10	20	30	40	50	60	70	80	90	100

Exercise A

Understanding the story. Answer each question by writing a complete sentence. Begin each sentence with a capital letter, and end each sentence with a period. You may use the line numbers in parentheses to help you.

1. Where did the boy decide to go? (1)

   To the neighboring village

2. What did the boy want to ask the priests? (2)

   if He could be His Assistant

3. Why was the temple closed? (5)

   Because a Goblin Had scared away the priests and Had taken possesion of the temple.

4. Why did the warriors go to the temple at night? (7)

   To Kill the gobling

5. Where was the temple? (13)

   on top of a large Hill at the end of the biggest street in village.

6. What did the boy see coming from inside the temple? (14)

   Light

7. What did the boy draw all over the screens? (34)

   Cats

8. What woke up the boy in the middle of the night? (43 or 44)

   A Horrible noise. Sound of fighting and screaming

9. How big was the goblin rat? (55)

   Bigger than a cow.

10. What killed the goblin? (61)

    the cat that he had drawn

Exercise B

Part A

Putting events in order. Put the events in the order in which they occurred. You may look back at the story.

1. _C_   — **a.** The boy saw the temple on top of a hill.

2. _a_   — **b.** He drew cats all over the screens.

3. _e_   — **c.** The boy walked to the next village.

4. _b_   — **d.** He saw a huge goblin rat.

5. _g_   — **e.** The boy knocked on the door and went in.

6. _f_   — **f.** He was awakened by loud noises.

7. _d_   — **g.** The boy fell asleep.

Part B

Now list the correct order of the events on the lines below.

1. the boy walked to the next village

2. the boy sow the temple on top of a Hill

3. the boy Knocked on the door and went in.

4. He drew cats all over the screens

5. the boy Fell sleep

6. He was awakened by loud noises.

7. He sow a huge gobline Rat

Exercise C

Adding vocabulary. On the left are 10 words from the story. Complete each sentence by adding the correct word.

✓ shelter

✓ creature

✓ curled

neighboring

✓ slid

✓ tempt

✓ silence

✓ famous

✓ peek

✓ spider

1. The temple was not far away. It was in a near, or _neighboring_, village.

2. The goblin wanted strangers to come to the temple. He kept on a light to _temp_ them there.

3. Sometimes people needed a place to stay for the night. Then they went to the temple for _shelter_.

4. The temple was filled with dust. There were _spider_ webs everywhere.

5. The closet had a sliding door. He _slid_ the door open.

6. The boy stepped into the small closet. Then he _curled_ up and went to sleep.

7. The boy heard noises. But he was afraid to open the door to _peek_ out.

8. For a long time he heard loud noises. Finally they stopped and there was _silence_.

9. He was the only thing alive in the temple. There was no other _creature_ there.

10. He is a very well known painter. He is _famous_.

Exercise D

Using verbs correctly. Fill in each blank using the **past tense** of the verb *to be* (*was, were*).

1. The boy did not know that the temple ___was___ closed.

2. He thought that there ___was___ some priests in the temple.

3. It ___was___ dark and all the people ___were___ asleep.

4. There ___was___ a light coming from the temple.

5. The boy heard sounds that ___were___ very loud.

6. There ___was___ dust everywhere in the temple.

7. There ___were___ some big white screens in the temple.

8. The noise ___was___ terrible.

9. The boy ___was___ afraid to move.

10. Their mouths ___were___ wet, and they ___were___ red with blood.

Begin each question by writing the **present tense** of the verb *to be* (*am, are, is*). Remember to use a capital letter.

11. ___Is___ the temple on top of a hill?

12. ___are___ there any priests in the temple?

13. ___Is___ the door of the temple locked?

14. "___am___ I safe here?" the boy asked himself.

15. ___Is___ the cats fighting with the rat?

Exercise E

Combining sentences. Combine the two sentences into one by using a comma and the **conjunction** (*but* or *so*) in parentheses. Write the sentence on the line. The first one has been done for you.

1. The temple was closed. The boy did not know this. (but)

   The temple was closed, but the boy did not know this.

2. The boy had never heard the story about the temple. He walked to the next village. (so)

   the boy Had never heard the story about the temple. So He walked to the next village.

   _____.

3. The boy knocked on the door. Nobody answered. (but)

   the boy Knocked on the door but Nobody answered.

   _____.

4. The door swung open. He went inside. (so)

   the door swung open so He went inside

   _____.

5. The boy looked around. He didn't see anyone. (but)

   the boy looked around but He didn't see anyone.

   _____.

6. He thought that a priest would arrive soon. He sat down and waited. (so)

He thought that a priest would arrive soon so He sat down and waited.

_____.

7. He was all alone. He began to feel frightened. (so)

He was all alone so He began to feel frightened.

_____.

8. The light in the temple went out. The terrible noise continued. (but)

the light in the temple went out but the terrible noise continued.

_____.

Exercise F

Vocabulary review. Write a complete sentence for each word or group of words.

1. silence ___the room was silence___

_____

_____

2. creature ___I love the different creature of the world.___

_____

3. neighboring ___the temple was not far away. It was in a near, or neighboring village.___

_____

4. tempt ___He kept on a light to temp them there.___

_____

5. curled _then He curled up and went to sleep._

6. peek _He was afraid to open the door to peek out_

7. spider _there were spider webs everywhere_

8. warrior _the warrior went to the temple to kill the golpin._

9. cautiously _the boy got out of His Hiding place cautiously._

10. look forward to _the boy look forward to meet the priest_

SHARING WITH OTHERS

Everyone can learn by sharing ideas. Meet with your partner or group to discuss these questions. Write your answer to one of the questions.

- ◆ The author makes everything in the story seem real. However, some things in the story could not have happened. List two things that might have taken place. List two things that could never have happened.
- ◆ At the end of the story, the boy finally understood "the power of his drawings." What was this "power"? How did it help make the boy a famous artist?

_____

_____

_____

_____

_____

_____

_____

_____

_____

_____

_____

_____

_____

_____

THE OPEN WINDOW

by Saki

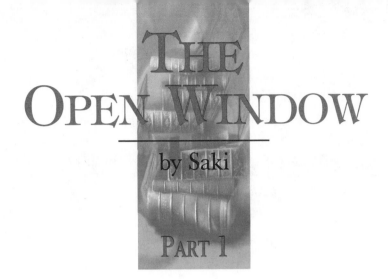

THE OPEN WINDOW

by Saki

PART 1

A French window is a large glass door. It usually opens onto a garden at the back of the house. As you will see, a French window plays an important part in this well-known story by Saki.

Framton Nuttel was sitting in a chair when the young lady entered the room.

"My aunt will be down in ten minutes," the young lady told Framton very calmly. "She asked me to wait here with you until then."

5   Framton wondered what to say to the fifteen-year-old girl. He felt nervous, very nervous. Strangers always made him feel nervous. *Waiting* made him feel nervous. *Talking* made him feel nervous. *Everything* made him feel nervous. In fact, he had come to the country to calm his nerves.

10   His sister had given him some advice. "I know just what you need," she had said. "Get away from the city for a while. A week in the country will be good for you. I'll give you the names of some nice people you can visit while you're there. Otherwise you'll stay in your room all the time. You won't say a word to anyone. Then your nerves
15   will get worse than ever."

Mrs. Sappleton was one of the "nice people" she recommended. Now Framton waited for her to come down from upstairs.

"Do you know many people around here?" the young lady finally asked. Her words broke a long silence.

20   "I don't know *any* of the people around here," Framton replied. "My sister visited this part of the country four years ago. She met your aunt, Mrs. Sappleton, then. My sister said that Mrs. Sappleton was . . . very nice."

"Then you don't know anything about my aunt?" the calm young
25   lady asked.

"Only her name and address," admitted Mr. Nuttel. He looked around the room and wondered whether or not Mrs. Sappleton was

married. Something about the room suggested that a man lived there.

"Her terrible **tragedy** happened exactly three years ago *today*!" said the girl. "Three years ago today. That was after your sister was here."

"Her tragedy?" asked Framton, nervously. It didn't seem possible that terrible things could happen in this quiet, peaceful place.

The niece pointed to a large French window that opened like a big door onto the lawn. She said, "You are probably wondering why we keep that window wide open on a day in October."

"It *is* very warm for this time of the year," said Framton. "But does that window have anything to do with the tragedy?"

"Yes," said the girl. "Just three years ago today, her husband and her two brothers went out through that window. They were going hunting. They never came back! All three drowned in a **swamp**. It had been a very rainy summer, you know, and places that had always been safe suddenly became dangerous. Their bodies were never found. That was the worst part of it."

Here the girl's voice began to crack. "Poor, dear aunt," said the girl. "She has never been able **to get over** what happened. She still believes that they will all come back some day—they and the little brown dog that went with them. She thinks they will walk in through that window the way they always did. That is why that window is kept open every day until it gets dark."

The girl shook her head sadly. "Poor aunt, she has often told me how they went out. Her husband had his white raincoat over his shoulder. And Ronnie, her younger brother, was singing, 'London Bridge is falling down, falling down.' He always sang that to tease her because she said it **got on her nerves**. Do you know, sometimes, on quiet evenings like this, I get a strange feeling that they will all walk in through that window—"

The girl suddenly began to shake, and she stopped talking. Framton was very glad to see the aunt enter the room.

Put an *x* in the box next to the correct answer.

Reading Comprehension

1. The young lady said that her aunt would come down
   - ❏ **a.** in a minute.
   - ☒ **b.** in ten minutes.
   - ❏ **c.** in an hour.

2. How old was the young lady?
   - ❏ **a.** five years old
   - ❏ **b.** ten years old
   - ☒ **c.** fifteen years old

3. Framton's sister told him to
   - ☒ **a.** go to the country for a week.
   - ❏ **b.** spend time in the city.
   - ❏ **c.** rest in his room.

4. When did Framton's sister meet Mrs. Sappleton?
   - ❏ **a.** four weeks ago
   - ❏ **b.** four months ago
   - ☒ **c.** four years ago

5. The window was kept wide open on a day in
   - ☒ **a.** October.
   - ❏ **b.** November.
   - ❏ **c.** December.

6. The girl said that Mrs. Sappleton's husband
   - ❏ **a.** was visiting some friends.
   - ☒ **b.** drowned while he was hunting.
   - ❏ **c.** would be home soon.

Vocabulary

7. Framton didn't think that a tragedy could happen in that quiet, peaceful place. The word *tragedy* means
   - ☒ **a.** something terrible.
   - ❏ **b.** something wonderful.
   - ❏ **c.** something funny.

8. She said that three people drowned in a swamp. What is a *swamp*?
   - ❏ **a.** a mountain
   - ❏ **b.** a valley
   - ☒ **c.** wet, soft land

Idioms

9. The aunt was not able to get over the accident. The idiom *to get over* means
   - ❏ **a.** to like or enjoy.
   - ❏ **b.** to recover from, or get used to.
   - ☒ **c.** to help or assist.

10. Mrs. Sappleton didn't like it when her brother sang because it got on her nerves. When something *gets on your nerves*, it
    - ❏ **a.** pleases you.
    - ☒ **b.** bothers you.
    - ❏ **c.** makes you very sad.

How many questions did you answer correctly? Circle your score. Then fill in your score on the Score Chart on page 184.

Number Correct	1	2	3	4	5	6	7	8	9	10
Score	10	20	30	40	50	60	70	80	90	100

Exercise A

Understanding the story. Answer each question by writing a complete sentence. Begin each sentence with a capital letter, and end each sentence with a period. You may use the line numbers in parentheses to help you.

1. Where was Framton when the young lady entered the room? (1)

   Was sitting in a chair

2. How old was the young lady? (5)

   Fifteen-year-old

3. Why had Framton come to the country? (8)

   to calm His nerves

4. When did Framton's sister visit that part of the country? (21)

   Four years ago

5. What did Framton know about the aunt? (26)

   Her name and address.

6. When did Mrs. Sappleton's tragedy happen? (29)

   Exactly three years ago.

7. What did the girl say happened to the husband and two brothers? (41)

   All three drowned in a swamp.

8. Why is the window kept open every day until it gets dark? (48)

   She think they will walk in through that window
   the way they always did.

9. What did the husband have over his shoulder? (52)

   His white Raincoat.

10. Why did Ronnie always sing, "London Bridge is falling down"? (54)

    to tease her

Exercise B

Part A

Putting events in order. Put the events in the order in which they occurred. You may look back at the story.

1. _g_
2. _c_
3. _a_
4. _b_
5. _d_
6. _f_
7. _e_

— **a.** The girl pointed to a large French window.

— **b.** She said that Mrs. Sappleton's husband and two brothers had drowned.

— **c.** When he saw the girl, Framton felt nervous.

d. She said that their bodies had never been found.

e. Framton was glad to see the aunt enter the room.

— **f.** She said that her aunt believes they will come back some day.

— **g.** The young lady entered the room.

Part B

Now list the correct order of the events on the lines below.

1. the young Lady entered the room.

2. When he saw the girl, Framton felt Nervous.

3. the girl Pointed to a large French window

4. She said that Mrs. Sappleton's Husband and two brothers Had growned.

5. She said that their bodies had never been Found.

6. She said that her aunt belives they will come back some say.

7. Framton was glad to see the aunt enter the room.

Exercise C

Adding vocabulary. On the left are 10 words from the story. Complete each sentence by adding the correct word.

niece

tease

advice

lawn (*pasto*)

nervous

dangerous

upstairs

recommended

shoulder

admitted

1. Framton Nuttel needed a rest because everything made him _Nervous_.

2. Framton's sister gave him some _Recommended_ about what to do.

3. His sister _Advice_ that he visit Mrs. Sappleton.

4. Framton was waiting for Mrs. Sappleton to come down from _upstairs_.

5. The _Niece_ said that her aunt would be there soon.

6. Framton _Admitted_ that he knew very little about the aunt.

7. The French window opened like a door onto the _Lawn_.

8. Places that had always been safe suddenly became _dangeRous_.

9. Ronnie liked to _tease_ his sister by singing when he got near the house.

10. Her husband had his raincoat over his _SHoulder_.

Exercise D

Using verbs correctly. Fill in the blanks in each sentence to form the **past perfect tense**. Use *had* plus the **past participle** of the verb in parentheses. The first one has been done for you.

1. Framton ___had___ ___come___ to the country to rest. (come)

2. His sister ___had___ ___give___ him the names of some people to visit. (give)

3. "I know just what you need," she ___had___ ___say___. (say)

4. Framton's sister ___had___ ___go___ to that part of the country a few years ago. (go)

5. She ___had___ ___see___ Mrs. Sappleton and her family. (see)

6. She ___had___ ___speak___ to Mrs. Sappleton then. (speak)

7. She ___had___ ___tell___ Framton to visit Mrs. Sappleton. (tell)

8. It ___had___ ___be___ a very rainy summer. (be)

9. Her husband ___had___ ___take___ his raincoat with him. (take)

10. Her younger brother ___had___ ___sing___. a song. (sing)

Exercise E

Adding punctuation. The following passage needs **punctuation marks**. Add capital letters, periods, question marks, commas, and quotation marks. Then write the corrected passage on the lines below.

the young lady looked at framton nuttel he stared back at her nobody said a word framton felt tired nervous bored, and unhappy then the young lady asked do you know many people who live around here do you know my aunt

_____

_____

_____

_____

_____

_____

_____

_____

_____

Exercise F

Vocabulary review. Write a complete sentence for each word or group of words.

1. dangerous _Places that had always been safe_ _suddenly become Dangerous._

2. niece _I called my niece Yesterday._

3. lawn _My Horses eat Lawn everyday_

4. upstairs _My note book is upstairs, and_ _I don't know How to get it._

5. nervous _I'm Feeling Nervous when I_ _drink coffe_

6. shoulder _my Friend Have broken His_ _Right Shoulder._

7. tease _I'm teasing my sister with_ _Her Husband._

8. tragedy _A friend of my Had a tragedy_ _last Saturday._

9. swamp _My three Friends drowned in_ _a Swamp._

10. gets on my nerves _A stranger alway make me_ _Feel Nervous._ /

SHARING WITH OTHERS

Everyone can learn by sharing ideas. Meet with your partner or group to discuss these questions. Write your answer to one of the questions.

◆ Everything made Framton Nuttel nervous. His sister suggested that he go to the country for a week. Suppose that you could give Framton some advice. What would you tell him?

◆ Why was Framton so glad to see the aunt enter the room? Give as many reasons as you can.

_____

_____

_____

_____

_____

_____

_____

_____

_____

_____

_____

_____

_____

PART 2

"I'm so sorry I'm late," the aunt apologized to Framton. "I hope that you enjoyed talking to Vera, my niece."

"She has been . . . uh . . . very interesting," said Framton.

"I hope you don't mind the open window," Mrs. Sappleton said
5 cheerfully. "My husband and my brothers will be back soon from hunting. They always like to come in through that window. They've been hunting in the swamp today, so they're sure to have mud on their boots." Mrs. Sappleton smiled and added, "They'll get mud all over my beautiful carpets. But that's the way you men are,
10 aren't you?"

She began to talk happily about hunting. To Framton it was **dreadful**. He was getting more and more nervous. He tried again and again to change the **conversation** to a different subject. But Mrs. Sappleton was not really listening to him. She was **keeping an**
15 **eye on** the open window and the lawn beyond it. It was certainly unlucky that he had come to visit that very day—just three years to the day when the awful accident took place.

Framton was talking to Mrs. Sappleton. "The doctors all agree that I should rest completely," Framton was saying. "Nothing should
20 upset me or make me nervous. I need to be calm and avoid excitement." Framton paused and then added, "The doctors do not agree about what foods I should eat."

"Really?" said Mrs. Sappleton, beginning to yawn. Then suddenly she sat up straight in her chair and looked bright and alert. But it
25 was not because of what Framton was saying.

"Here they are at last!" she exclaimed. "They're just in time to have tea. And, as I thought, they have mud all over their boots."

Framton shivered slightly. He shook his head sadly and turned to the niece to give her a look of pity.

30 But the girl was staring out through the open window. Her eyes were wide with horror. A **chill** went up Framton's back as he turned

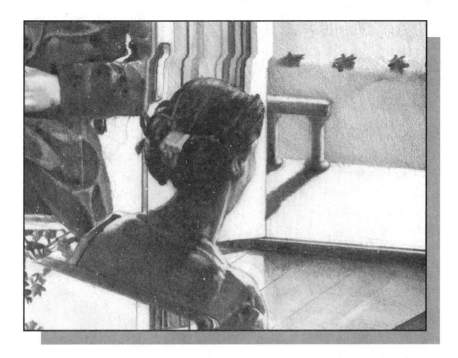

around in fear. He looked out the open window.

In the dim light, three figures were walking across the lawn toward the window. They all carried guns under their arms, and one of them had a white raincoat around his shoulders. A tired brown dog stayed close to their heels. Without making a sound, they moved closer to the house. Then a young voice began to sing, "London Bridge is falling down, falling down. . . ."

Framton grabbed his hat and ran wildly out of the house. Someone riding a bicycle had to drive into a bush to keep from hitting him.

"Here we are, my dear," said the man with the white raincoat, as he came in the window. "I don't think that we're too muddy. Who was that man who rushed out as we came by?"

"A very strange man, a Mr. Nuttel," said Mrs. Sappleton. "He could only talk about how ill he was. Then he ran away without saying a word when you arrived. One would think he had seen a ghost!"

"I think I know the reason," Vera said very calmly. "It was probably the dog. He told me he had a terrible fear of dogs. He said he was once chased into a cemetery by a pack of hungry dogs. He said he had to spend the night in a newly dug grave while the dogs stood a few feet above him barking and snarling and growling. That would make anyone nervous."

"That's true," said the aunt.

Vera *loved* to make up stories. As you can see, she was very good at doing that!

Put an *x* in the box next to the correct answer.

Reading Comprehension

1. Mrs. Sappleton said that her husband and brothers
   - ❏ **a.** had died.
   - ❏ **b.** were shopping.
   - ☒ **c.** would be home soon.

2. Which statement is true?
   - ❏ **a.** The aunt listened carefully to what Framton was saying.
   - ☒ **b.** The aunt wasn't really listening to Framton.
   - ❏ **c.** The aunt thought Framton was very interesting.

3. Framton's doctors said he should
   - ☒ **a.** rest.
   - ❏ **b.** work harder.
   - ❏ **c.** spend more time in the city.

4. The three men were carrying
   - ❏ **a.** raincoats.
   - ☒ **b.** guns.
   - ❏ **c.** umbrellas.

5. Vera said that Framton ran away because he
   - ☒ **a.** thought he saw a ghost.
   - ❏ **b.** did not like Mrs. Sappleton's husband.
   - ❏ **c.** was afraid of the dog.

6. Vera loved to
   - ❏ **a.** help her aunt.
   - ☒ **b.** make up stories.
   - ❏ **c.** watch television.

Vocabulary

7. The aunt kept talking about hunting. Framton thought that was dreadful. The word *dreadful* means
   - ☒ **a.** terrible.
   - ❏ **b.** wonderful.
   - ❏ **c.** helpful.

8. He kept trying to change the conversation. The word *conversation* means
   - ❏ **a.** food.
   - ❏ **b.** house.
   - ☒ **c.** talk.

9. A chill went up Framton's back as he turned around in fear. When you have a *chill*, you feel
   - ❏ **a.** hot.
   - ☒ **b.** cold.
   - ❏ **c.** sad.

Idioms

10. Mrs. Sappleton was keeping an eye on the open window. The idiom *to keep an eye on* means
    - ☒ **a.** to watch.
    - ❏ **b.** to break.
    - ❏ **c.** to speak.

How many questions did you answer correctly? Circle your score. Then fill in your score on the Score Chart on page 184.

Number Correct	1	2	3	4	5	6	7	8	9	10
Score	10	20	30	40	50	60	70	80	90	100

Exercise A

Understanding the story. Answer each question by writing a complete sentence. Begin each sentence with a capital letter, and end each sentence with a period. You may use the line numbers in parentheses to help you.

1. Who liked to come in through the open window? (6)

   My husband and my brothers will be back soon from hunting.

2. What did Mrs. Sappleton talk about? (11)

   She began to talk happily About Hunting.

3. What was Mrs. Sappleton looking at? (14)

   the open window and the lawn beyond it.

4. How long ago did the awful accident take place? (16)

   three years Ago.

5. What did the doctors agree that Framton should do? (18)

   Rest completly.

6. Who was walking across the lawn toward the window? (33)

   three Figures. And A Doce.

7. What were the men carrying under their arms? (34)

   they all carry Guns

8. What did Framton do when he heard someone singing? (39)

   grabbed his hat and ran wildly out of the House.

9. What did Mrs. Sappleton say that Framton talked about? (46)

   How ill he was

10. What reason did Vera give to explain why Framton ran away? (50)

    it was probably the dog.

Exercise B

Part A

Putting events in order. Put the events in the order in which they occurred. You may look back at the story.

1. C
2. b
3. a
4. f
5. ___
6. ___
7. ___

— **a.** She said that her husband and brothers would be back soon.

— **b.** Suddenly Mrs. Sappleton sat up straight in her chair.

— **c.** Mrs. Sappleton came into the room.

d. Vera said she knew why Framton ran away.

e. "Here they are at last!" she exclaimed.

— **f.** Framton explained that he needed to rest.

g. Framton ran wildly out of the house.

Part B

Now list the correct order of the events on the lines below.

1. _____

2. _____

   _____

3. _____

4. _____

   _____

5. _____

6. _____

7. _____

Exercise C

Adding vocabulary. On the left are 10 words from the story. Complete each sentence by adding the correct word.

yawn

dim

carpets

alert

apologized

pity

snarling

pack

figures

accident

1. Mrs. Sappleton arrived late, so she _Apologized_ to Framton.

2. She was afraid that the men would get mud all over her beautiful _CARPETS_.

3. Vera said that the men died in a terrible _Accident_.

4. Mrs. Sappleton suddenly sat up in her chair and looked bright and _Alert_.

5. Framton shook his head sadly and gave the girl a look of _pity_.

6. Since she was not interested in what Framton was saying, Mrs. Sappleton began to _Yawn_.

7. Late in the day, the light becomes _Dim_.

8. They saw three _Figures_ walking toward the house.

9. He was once chased by a _pack_ of hungry dogs.

10. The dogs stood a few feet away, barking and _snarling_.

Exercise D

Using verbs correctly. Fill in each blank using the **present tense** of the verb *to have* (*have, has*).

1. Mrs. Sappleton ___has___ beautiful carpets.

2. Mr. and Mrs. Sappleton ___have___ a house in the country.

3. The hunters ___have___ guns.

4. Mrs. Sappleton ___has___ a niece named Vera.

5. The men ___has___ mud all over their boots.

6. Mrs. Sappleton's brother, Ronnie, ___have___ a very good voice.

7. Vera said that Framton ___has___ a fear of dogs.

8. The brothers ___have___ a little brown dog.

9. Mr. Sappleton ___has___ a new, white raincoat.

10. When they return from hunting, the hunters ___have___ tea.

11. Vera ___has___ fun making up stories.

12. "The Open Window" ___has___ a surprising ending.

Exercise E

Putting words in correct order. Unscramble each sentence by putting the words in the correct order. Add *s* to the verb when necessary. Write each sentence on the line. The first one has been done for you. Each sentence is in the **present tense**.

1. story / This / tell / man / named Framton / a / about

   This story tells about a man named Framton.

2. visit / Mrs. Sappleton / woman / named / a / He

   _____.

3. dead / are / say / Vera / husband and brothers / Mrs. Sappleton's / that

   _____

   _____.

4. Framton / the / window / through / them / see / Suddenly

   _____

   _____.

5. come / closer and closer / They / house / to / the

   _____.

6. grab / run / hat / his / Framton / and / away

   _____.

7. wonder / why / They / Framton / out / rushed

   _____.

8. the dog / was / he / of / Vera / say / afraid

   _____.

9. stories / Vera / love / to / up / make

   _____.

Now look at the sentences you wrote. Underline the verb or verbs in the **present tense** in each sentence.

Exercise F

Vocabulary review. Write a complete sentence for each word or group of words.

1. accident _____

_____

2. apologized _____

_____

3. carpets _____

_____

4. snarling _____

_____

5. yawn _____

_____

6. dim _____

_____

7. alert _____

_____

8. dreadful _____

_____

9. conversation _____

_____

10. keeping an eye on _____

_____

SHARING WITH OTHERS

Everyone can learn by sharing ideas. Meet with your partner or group to discuss these questions. Write your answer to one of the questions.

◆ Vera "loved to make up stories." Think about the two stories Vera made up in "The Open Window." Which one do you think she liked better? Why?

◆ Suppose that you are Framton and that you are telling your sister about your visit to the country. What would you say?

_____

_____

_____

_____

_____

_____

_____

_____

_____

_____

_____

_____

_____

SHOES FOR HECTOR

by Nicholasa Mohr

SHOES FOR HECTOR

by Nicholasa Mohr

PART 1

This story was written more than twenty years ago. Twenty-five dollars bought a lot more then than it does today.

•

Hector's mother had gone to see Uncle Luis the day before graduation, and he had come by the same evening. Everyone sat in the living room watching Uncle Luis as he took a white box out of a brown paper bag. Opening the box, he removed a pair of shiny, light-brown
5   shoes with tall heels and narrow, pointed toes. Holding them up proudly, he said, "This cost me 12 bucks, boy!"

Everybody looked at Hector and then back at Uncle Luis.

"Here you go, my boy . . ." He gestured toward Hector. "Try them on."

"I'm not gonna try *those* things on!" Hector said.

10   "Why not?" asked Uncle Luis. "What's wrong with them? They are the latest style, man. Listen, boy, you will be *a la moda*[1] with these."

"They . . . they're just not my type. Besides, they don't **go with** my suit—it's navy blue. Those shoes are orange!" Hector's younger brothers and sister looked at each other and began to giggle and laugh.

15   "Shut up, you dummies!" Hector shouted angrily.

"Hector, what is the matter with you?" his mother asked. "That's no way to behave."

"I'd rather wear my sneakers than those, Mami. You and Papi promised to buy me shoes. You didn't say anything about wearing
20   Uncle Luis's shoes."

"Wait a minute, now. Just a minute," Hector's father said. "We know, but we just couldn't manage it now. Since your Uncle Luis has the same size foot as you, and he was nice enough to lend you his new shoes, what's the difference? We did what we could, son; you have to
25   be satisfied."

---

1. *a la moda:* the Spanish words for "in style."

Hector felt the blood rushing to his face and tried to control
his embarrassment and anger. His parents had been preparing his
graduation party now for more than a week. "They should have spent
the money on my shoes instead of on a dumb party," he thought.
Hector had used up all the earnings from his part-time job. He had
bought his suit, tie, shirt, socks, and handkerchief. His parents had
promised to buy him the shoes. "There is not one cent left," he
thought, and it was just too late now.

"It's not my fault that they laid me off for three days," his father
said, "and that Petie got sick and that Georgie needed a winter jacket
and Juanito some . . ."

As his father spoke, Hector wanted to say a few things. Like, "No,
it's my fault that you had to spend the money for shoes on a party and
a cake and everything to **impress** the neighbors and the *familia*. Stupid
dinner!" But instead he remained quiet, looking down at the floor, and
did not say a word.

"Hector . . . come on, my son. Hector, try them on, *bendito*.[2] Uncle
Luis was nice enough to bring them," he heard his mother plead.
"Please, for me."

"Maybe I can get into Papi's shoes," Hector answered.

"My shoes don't fit you. And your brothers are all younger and
smaller than you. There's nobody else. You are lucky Uncle Luis has
the same size foot," his father responded.

"Okay, I'll just wear my sneakers," said Hector.

2. *bendito:* the Spanish word for "dear."

50   "Oh, no . . . no, never mind. You can't wear sneakers. You wear those shoes!" his mother said.

"Mami, they are *orange*!" Hector responded. "And look at the pointed fronts—they go on for a mile. I'm not wearing them!"

"Come on, please," his mother **coaxed**. "They look nice and brand 55 new too."

"Hector!" his father said loudly. "Now, your Uncle Luis was nice enough to bring them, and you are going to try them on." Everyone was silent and Hector sat **sulking**. His mother took the shoes from Uncle Luis and went over to Hector.

60   "Here, son, try them on, at least. See?" She held them up. "Look at them. They are not orange, just a light-brown color, that's all. Only a very light brown."

Without looking at anyone, Hector took the shoes and slowly put them on. No doubt about it, they felt like a perfect fit.

65   "How about that?" Uncle Luis smiled. "Now you look sharp. Right in style, boy!"

Hector stood up and walked a few paces. In spite of all the smiling faces in the living room, Hector still heard all the remarks he was sure his friends would make if he wore those shoes.

70   "Okay, you look wonderful. And it's only for one morning. You can take them right off after graduation," his mother said gently.

Hector removed the shoes and put them back in the box, resigned that there was just no way out. At that moment he even found himself wishing that he had not been selected as valedictorian[3] and wishing he 75 wasn't receiving any honors.

"Take your time, Hector. You don't have to give them back to me right away. Wear the shoes for the party. So you look good," he heard Uncle Luis calling out as he walked into his bedroom.

"That stupid party!" Hector whispered out loud.

3. *valedictorian*: the student who has the highest average in his or her
    class. The valedictorian usually makes a speech at graduation.

Put an *x* in the box next to the correct answer.

Reading Comprehension

1. Who gave Hector the shoes?
   - ❑ **a.** Hector's mother
   - ❑ **b.** Hector's father
   - ❑ **c.** Uncle Luis

2. How much did the shoes cost?
   - ❑ **a.** 10 dollars
   - ❑ **b.** 12 dollars
   - ❑ **c.** 20 dollars

3. Hector did not like the shoes because
   - ❑ **a.** they were too big.
   - ❑ **b.** they were too small.
   - ❑ **c.** they looked orange.

4. His parents spent money for
   - ❑ **a.** a party for Hector.
   - ❑ **b.** a new suit.
   - ❑ **c.** a shirt and tie.

5. Hector was afraid that his friends would
   - ❑ **a.** stay away from his party.
   - ❑ **b.** make fun of his shoes.
   - ❑ **c.** be angry with his parents.

6. Which statement is true?
   - ❑ **a.** Hector wasn't receiving any honors at graduation.
   - ❑ **b.** Hector was the class valedictorian.
   - ❑ **c.** Hector didn't have any brothers or sisters.

Vocabulary

7. Hector's mother wanted him to wear the shoes. "Please, for me," she coaxed. The word *coaxed* means
   - ❑ **a.** asked sweetly.
   - ❑ **b.** shouted loudly.
   - ❑ **c.** thought about.

8. The unhappy Hector sat sulking. The word *sulking* means
   - ❑ **a.** answering questions.
   - ❑ **b.** looking sad.
   - ❑ **c.** playing cheerfully.

9. Hector thought that his parents spent the money to impress their neighbors. When you *impress* people, you
   - ❑ **a.** make them feel strongly about something.
   - ❑ **b.** don't care what they think.
   - ❑ **c.** borrow something from them.

Idioms

10. Hector said the shoes "don't go with my suit." The idiom *to go with* means
    - ❑ **a.** to move slowly.
    - ❑ **b.** to go away.
    - ❑ **c.** to look good with.

How many questions did you answer correctly? Circle your score. Then fill in your score on the Score Chart on page 184.

Number Correct	1	2	3	4	5	6	7	8	9	10
Score	10	20	30	40	50	60	70	80	90	100

EXERCISES TO HELP YOU

Exercise A

Understanding the story. Answer each question by writing a complete sentence. Begin each sentence with a capital letter, and end each sentence with a period. You may use the line numbers in parentheses to help you.

1. When had Hector's mother gone to see Uncle Luis? (1)

   _____

2. Where did everyone sit while they watched Uncle Luis? (2)

   _____

3. What did Uncle Luis remove from the box? (4)

   _____

4. How much did the shoes cost? (6)

   _____

5. What color was Hector's suit? (13)

   _____

6. How long had Hector's parents been preparing his party? (27)

   _____

   _____

7. What had Hector bought with his earnings? (31)

   _____

   _____

8. What had Hector's mother and father promised to buy him? (32)

   _____

9. How did the shoes fit? (64)

   _____

10. What did Hector whisper out loud? (79)

   _____

Exercise B

Part A

Putting events in order. Put the events in the order in which they occurred. You may look back at the story.

1. ____

2. ____

3. ____

4. ____

5. ____

6. ____

7. ____

a. Hector's mother told Hector to wear the shoes.

b. Uncle Luis took some shoes out of a box.

c. Hector slowly put the shoes on.

d. Hector took off the shoes and put them back in the box.

e. Hector said that he didn't want to wear the shoes.

f. Hector stood up and took a few steps with the shoes.

g. Uncle Luis asked Hector to try on the shoes.

Part B

Now list the correct order of the events on the lines below.

1. _____

2. _____

3. _____

4. _____

_____

5. _____

6. _____

_____

7. _____

_____

Exercise C

Adding vocabulary. On the left are 10 words from the story. Complete each sentence by adding the correct word.

earnings

behave

graduation

satisfied

giggle

promised

remarks

gestured

plead

embarrassment

1. Hector's brothers and sister smiled. Then they began to _____ and laugh.

2. Hector's mother went to see Uncle Luis the day before Hector's _____.

3. Hector had a part-time job. He bought some clothing with his _____.

4. Uncle Luis pointed to the box. "Try them on," he said, as he _____ toward the shoes.

5. "Try the shoes on. *Please* try them on," his mother began to _____.

6. Hector was worried about what his friends might say. He was worried about the _____ they might make.

7. Hector's mother didn't like what Hector was doing. She told him, "That's no way to _____."

8. Hector's parents had _____ to buy him new shoes.

9. Hector's parents thought that Hector should be happy with what they did. They thought that he should be _____ .

10. Hector believed that everyone was going to laugh at him. Then he would have to hide his shame and _____.

Exercise D

Using verbs correctly. Change each **positive sentence** to a **negative sentence** by using *didn't* plus the correct form of the verb. The first one has been done for you.

1. Uncle Luis sat in the living room.

   Uncle Luis didn't sit in the living room.

2. Uncle Luis took a box out of a paper bag.

   _____.

3. Uncle Luis held up a pair of shoes.

   _____.

4. Hector's parents spent money for a party for Hector.

   _____

   _____.

5. Hector bought a shirt, a tie, and socks.

   _____.

6. Uncle Luis gave Hector a pair of shoes.

   _____.

7. Uncle Luis brought the shoes in a box.

   _____.

8. Hector felt very angry.

   _____.

9. Hector thought that his friends would make fun of him.

   _____

   _____.

10. His mother said that the shoes were light brown.

    _____.

11. Hector's father spoke to Hector about the shoes.

    _____.

12. Hector had to wear the shoes to graduation.

    _____.

Exercise E

Using nouns with irregular plurals. Some nouns have irregular plural forms. Use the chart to help you fill in the correct plural form in each sentence below. Use each word once. The first one has been done for you.

Singular	Plural
woman	women
man	men
child	children
foot	feet
knife	knives
loaf	loaves
wife	wives
leaf	leaves

1. Uncle Luis and Hector had the same size foot. Their

   ___*feet*___ were the same size.

2. Hector's mother has more than one child. She has five

   _____.

3. Hector's father bought a loaf of bread. Then he returned to the

   store and bought two more _____.

4. When Hector's brothers grow up, they will be _____.

5. When girls grow up, they will be _____.

6. Outside, a leaf was falling to the ground. The ground was already

   covered with _____.

7. There was a knife next to each plate. Altogether there were seven

   _____.

8. Husbands and _____ were invited to the graduation party.

Exercise F

Vocabulary review. Write a complete sentence for each word or group of words.

1. giggle _____

_____

2. earnings _____

_____

3. satisfied _____

_____

4. behave _____

_____

5. promised _____

_____

6. gestured _____

_____

7. graduation _____

_____

8. coaxed _____

_____

9. sulking _____

_____

10. doesn't go with _____

_____

SHARING WITH OTHERS

Everyone can learn by sharing ideas. Meet with your partner or group to discuss these questions. Write your answer to one of the questions.

◆ Hector hated the light-brown shoes. He said that he would rather wear his sneakers to graduation. Do you think that Hector would *really* have worn sneakers to school on Graduation Day? Give reasons for your answer.

◆ Some people always need to be "in style." Others don't care very much about the clothing they wear. Which group are you in—or are you somewhere in between? Explain your answer.

_____

_____

_____

_____

_____

_____

_____

_____

_____

_____

_____

_____

_____

_____

PART 2

With a pained expression on his face the next morning, Hector left his apartment wearing Uncle Luis's shoes. His mother and father walked proudly with him.

Hector arrived at the school auditorium and took his place in line. Smiling and waving at him, his parents sat in the audience.

"Hector López . . ." He walked up the long **aisle** onto the stage. He finished his speech and sat on a chair provided for him on the stage. They called his name again several times, and each time Hector received an honor or prize. Included were a wristwatch and a check for cash. Whenever Hector stood up and walked to the podium,[1] he prayed that no one would notice his shoes.

Finally, graduation exercises were over and Hector hurried off the stage, looking for his parents. People congratulated him on his many honors and on his speech. His school friends shook his hand and they exchanged addresses. Hector found himself engaged in long good-byes. Slowly, people began to leave the large auditorium, and Hector and his parents headed for home.

Hector sat on his bed and took off Uncle Luis's shoes. "Good-bye," he said out loud, **making a face**, and dropped them into the box. He sighed with relief. "No one had even **mentioned** the shoes," he thought. "Man . . . I bet they didn't even notice them. Boy! Was I ever lucky . . . Nobody said a word. How about that?" he said to himself. Reaching under the bed, he took out his sneakers and happily put them on. "Never again," he continued, "if I can help it. No, sir. I'm gonna make sure I have shoes to wear!" He remembered all the things he had won at graduation. Looking at his new wristwatch, he put it on. "That's really something," he thought. He took out the check for cash he had received and read, "*Pay to the*

1. *podium:* part of the stage that is higher than the rest of the stage; the raised part of the stage.

Order of Hector López . . . The Sum of Twenty-Five Dollars and 00/100
Cents. I can't wait to show everybody," he said to himself.

Hector left his room and looked into the kitchen. His mother and
grandmother were busily preparing more food. He heard voices and
music in the living room and quickly walked in that direction. When
his younger brothers and sister saw him, they jumped up and down.

"Here's Hector!" Petie yelled.

"Happy Graduation Day, Hector!" everyone shouted.

The living room was full of people. His father was talking to
Uncle Luis and some neighbors. Uncle Luis called out, "There he is.
Hector! . . . There's my man now."

"Look." Hector's father pointed to a table that was loaded with
platters of food and a large cake. The cake had the **inscription**
"Happy Graduation to Hector." Behind the cake was a large card
printed in bright colors:

> HAPPY GRADUATION DAY, HECTOR
> FROM ALL YOUR FAMILY
> Mami, Papi, Abuelita, Petie, Georgie,
> Juanito, and Millie

Rows of colored crepe-paper streamers were strung across the ceiling and walls. Lots of balloons had been blown up and attached to each streamer. A big bell made of bright-red crepe paper and cardboard was set up under the center ceiling light. The record player was going full blast; some of the kids were busy dancing. Hector's face flushed when he saw Gloria. He had hoped she would come to the party, and there she was, looking great.

Some neighbors came over and congratulated Hector. His friends began to gather around, asking him lots of questions and admiring his wristwatch.

"Show them the check, Hector," his father said proudly. "That's some smart boy; he just kept getting honors! Imagine, they even gave him money. . . ."

Hector reached into his jacket pocket and took out the check for twenty-five dollars. He passed it around so that everyone could see it. Impressed, they asked him, "Hey, man. Hector, what you gonna do with all that money?"

"Yeah. Tell us, Hector, what you gonna do?"

Hector smiled and shrugged his shoulders. "Buy a pair of shoes! Any color except orange!" he replied.

Put an *x* in the box next to the correct answer.

Reading Comprehension

1. Which one of the following did Hector receive?
   - ❏ **a.** a wristwatch
   - ❏ **b.** a ring
   - ❏ **c.** fifty dollars in cash

2. Which statement is true?
   - ❏ **a.** Hector didn't win any prizes at graduation.
   - ❏ **b.** Hector was afraid that people would look at his shoes.
   - ❏ **c.** Hector was sorry to see Gloria at his party.

3. Hector received a check for
   - ❏ **a.** twenty-five dollars.
   - ❏ **b.** fifty-five dollars.
   - ❏ **c.** seventy-five dollars.

4. Hector's family was
   - ❏ **a.** angry with Hector.
   - ❏ **b.** very proud of Hector.
   - ❏ **c.** surprised that so many neighbors came to the party.

5. What did Hector plan to buy with the check?
   - ❏ **a.** a new shirt
   - ❏ **b.** some ties
   - ❏ **c.** a pair of shoes

Vocabulary

6. Hector walked up the aisle. What is an *aisle*?
   - ❏ **a.** a long, narrow space between rows of seats
   - ❏ **b.** some tables and chairs
   - ❏ **c.** a grassy field

7. They saw platters of food. The word *platters* means
   - ❏ **a.** cakes.
   - ❏ **b.** bottles.
   - ❏ **c.** large dishes.

8. The cake had the inscription, "Happy Graduation to Hector." What is an *inscription*?
   - ❏ **a.** words that are written on something
   - ❏ **b.** something good to eat
   - ❏ **c.** a wonderful party

9. No one mentioned his shoes. The word *mentioned* means
   - ❏ **a.** spoke about.
   - ❏ **b.** stepped on.
   - ❏ **c.** bought.

Idioms

10. Hector made a face and dropped the shoes. When you *make a face*, you
    - ❏ **a.** are hungry.
    - ❏ **b.** don't like something.
    - ❏ **c.** feel sleepy.

How many questions did you answer correctly? Circle your score. Then fill in your score on the Score Chart on page 184.

Number Correct	1	2	3	4	5	6	7	8	9	10
Score	10	20	30	40	50	60	70	80	90	100

Exercise A

Understanding the story. Answer each question by writing a complete sentence. Begin each sentence with a capital letter, and end each sentence with a period. You may use the line numbers in parentheses to help you.

1. Who walked proudly with Hector? (2)

_____

2. What happened each time they called Hector's name? (9)

_____

3. What were some of the things that Hector received? (9)

_____

4. Where did Hector drop Uncle Luis's shoes? (19)

_____

5. The check was for how much money? (29)

_____

6. Who was preparing more food in the kitchen? (31)

_____

_____

7. What did Hector's younger brothers and sister do when they saw him? (34)

_____

8. Who did Hector hope would come to the party? (53)

_____

9. What did Hector take out of his jacket pocket? (61)

_____

10. What was Hector going to buy? (66)

_____

Exercise B

Part A

Putting events in order. Put the events in the order in which they occurred. You may look back at the story.

1. ____

2. ____

3. ____

4. ____

5. ____

6. ____

7. ____

    a. Hector received a wristwatch and a check.

    b. Hector said he was going to buy a pair of shoes.

    c. Hector and his parents walked home.

    d. Hector passed around the check so that everyone could see it.

    e. Hector finished his speech and sat on a chair on the stage.

    f. Hector walked to the school with his parents.

    g. Everyone shouted, "Happy Graduation Day, Hector!"

Part B

Now list the correct order of the events on the lines below.

1. _____

2. _____

   _____

3. _____

4. _____

5. _____

   _____

6. _____

   _____

7. _____

Exercise C

Adding vocabulary. On the left are 10 words from the story. Complete each sentence by adding the correct word.

shrugged

auditorium

expression

ceiling

provided

audience

congratulated

exchanged

admiring

honor

1. When Hector arrived at the school

    _____, he took his place in line.

2. People _____ Hector for the prizes

    he had won.

3. Friends gathered around Hector and began

    _____ his watch.

4. Hector was not happy to wear the shoes; he had a

    sad _____ on his face.

5. Hector's mother and father were part of the

    _____ that watched the graduation.

6. Each time they called Hector's name, he received an

    _____.

7. Hector and his friends gave each other their

    addresses; they _____ addresses.

8. After Hector finished his speech, he sat on a chair

    that had been _____ for him.

9. When they asked Hector what he was going to do

    with the money, he _____ his shoulders.

10. Lots of bright balloons were hanging from the

    _____.

Exercise D

Using verbs correctly. Fill in the blanks in each sentence to form the **past continuous tense**. Use *was* or *were* plus the **present participle** (the *-ing* form) of the verb in parentheses. Some examples are *was singing, were laughing, was* not *running.* The first sentence has been done for you.

1. Hector ___was___ ___wearing___ Uncle Luis's shoes. (wear)

2. His parents _____ _____ proudly with him. (walk)

3. Hector _____ _____ that no one would see his shoes. (hope)

4. Hector's parents _____ _____ and smiling at him. (laugh)

5. Hector's friends _____ _____ him questions. (ask)

6. Hector's mother and grandmother _____ _____ more food. (prepare)

7. Uncle Luis _____ _____ to some neighbors. (talk)

8. His father _____ _____ to a cake on the table. (point)

9. Some of the kids _____ busy _____. (dance)

10. They _____ _____ themselves. (enjoy)

11. Large balloons _____ _____ from the walls. (hang)

12. Music _____ _____ loudly. (play)

13. Hector _____ _____ at his wristwatch. (look)

14. Some of the people _____ _____ good-bye. (say)

15. Hector _____ not _____ to buy a pair of orange shoes. (go)

Write your own sentences in the **past continuous tense** by using the verbs in parentheses.

16. (was listening) _____

    _____

17. (were shouting) _____

    _____

18. (was planning) _____

_____

19. (was not trying) _____

_____

20. (were not looking) _____

_____

Exercise E

Picking a pronoun. Fill in each blank by adding the correct **pronoun.**
Use each pronoun once.

I, me	we, us
you	you
he, she, it	they
him, her	them

1. After the graduation exercises were over, Hector found his parents

   and went home with _____.

2. Hector's father told Hector, "When your mother and I saw you on

   stage, _____ were very proud of _____.

3. Every time they called Hector's name, _____ gave _____
   a prize.

4. Hector's friends wanted to look at the check for cash. "Show

   _____ the check," they said.

5. Hector took out the check and passed _____ around.

6. "This is the wristwatch they gave _____," Hector said.

7. When Uncle Luis saw Hector, _____ called out, "There's
   Hector now!"

8 Hector was glad to see Gloria. He had hoped that _____ would
   come to the party.

9. Hector was looking for his mother. He saw _____ in the
   kitchen.

10. Hector told his parents, "_____ want to thank _____ for
    making a wonderful graduation party."

Exercise F

Vocabulary review. Write a complete sentence for each word or group
of words.

1. audience _____

_____

2. congratulated _____

_____

3. shrugged _____

_____

4. ceiling _____

_____

5. auditorium _____

_____

6. aisle _____

_____

7. platters _____

_____

8. inscription _____

_____

9. mentioned _____

_____

10. making a face _____

_____

SHARING WITH OTHERS

Everyone can learn by sharing ideas. Meet with your partner or group to discuss these questions. Write your answer to one of the questions.

◆ The Graduation Day speaker usually offers some words of advice. What advice do you think Hector might have given the other students? Think about what Hector might have said. Then write the first paragraph of Hector's speech.

◆ Hector was part of a very loving family. Do you agree or disagree with this statement? Give examples to support your answer.

_____

_____

_____

_____

_____

_____

_____

_____

_____

_____

_____

_____

_____

THE NECKLACE

by Guy de Maupassant

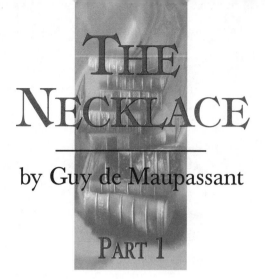

THE NECKLACE

by Guy de Maupassant

PART 1

A young French woman is the main character in "The Necklace."
This is one of the most famous short stories ever written.

Matilda was a pretty and charming young woman, but her family was very poor. She had no way of meeting a rich and **distinguished** man, so she married a clerk at the Department of Education.

Matilda was unhappy and suffered terribly. She was unhappy
5 because she thought she was born to enjoy the luxuries of life. She dreamed of having fine gowns and jewels. She longed for a beautiful house with servants. She imagined herself talking to rich and famous people.

Yet her own husband, Mr. Loisel, was hardly a rich and famous
10 man. At dinner he would lift the lid of a pot and say, "Ah, you've made some stew. There's nothing I like more than a good stew." And she would be dreaming about delicious dinners served on beautiful plates with expensive silverware.

But she had no fine dresses, no jewels, nothing. She dressed
15 simply because she could not afford to dress well. She disliked the apartment she lived in. She hated its dirty walls and worn-out chairs and ugly curtains. She thought that she deserved better things.

She had a friend, Jeanne Forester, who was rich. They were classmates years ago. But Matilda visited her friend less and less
20 these days. Matilda always felt very poor when she returned to her own apartment.

One evening Mr. Loisel came home with a big smile on his face.

"Here," he said, handing Matilda an envelope. "Here is something you will like."

25 She eagerly opened the envelope and pulled out a little card. On it were printed these words:

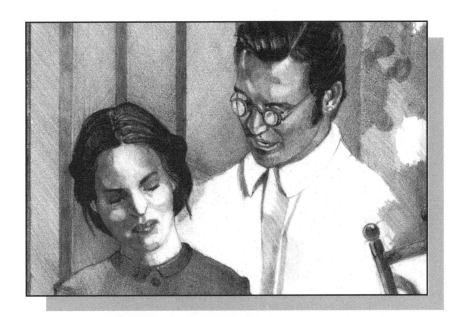

**The Minister of Education and His Wife
Invite You to a Party
Monday Evening, January 18
At the Minister's House**

Instead of being delighted, as her husband had hoped, Matilda frowned and tossed the invitation on the table.

"What do you expect me to do with that?" she asked.

30 "But my dear," said Mr. Loisel, "I thought you would be pleased. You don't go out very often, and this is a special event. Many important people will be there. I had a lot of trouble getting the invitation."

She looked at him and said, annoyed, "And what do you expect me to wear to the party?"

35 He had not thought about that. "Why," he said, "what about the green dress you sometimes wear. That looks very pretty to me. You could—"

He suddenly stopped talking, for he saw that his wife was beginning to cry. Two tears moved slowly down her face.

40 "What's the matter?" he asked anxiously.

She wiped her wet cheeks with the back of her hand.

"Nothing," she said, trying to calm herself. "Only I have no gown, and therefore I cannot go to the party. Give your invitation to some friend whose wife has good clothes."

45 He was hurt but he said, "Let's see, Matilda. How much would a new gown cost, something simple that you could wear again?"

Matilda thought about this for a few seconds. She was wondering how much she could ask for without frightening her **thrifty** husband.

Finally she said slowly, "I do not know the exact amount, but it seems to me that four hundred francs would be enough."

He turned pale. He had saved just that amount to buy a rifle so that he could go on a hunting trip with some friends next summer. But he said, "Very well. I will give you four hundred francs. But make sure that you buy something very pretty."

The party was only a few days away. Matilda's gown was ready, but she seemed sad, troubled, uneasy. Her husband said to her one evening, "What is the matter, Matilda? You've been acting so strangely the last few days."

She said, "I am upset because I don't have any jewelry to wear with my gown. I shall look so poor. I think that I'd rather not go to the party after all."

"Why don't you wear some flowers?" he suggested. "They're so fresh this time of the year. For ten francs you can get two or three beautiful roses."

This did not convince her. "No," she said, "there's nothing more embarrassing than to look poor among women who are rich."

He suddenly exclaimed, "How foolish we are! Ask your friend, Jeanne Forester, to lend you some jewels. You know her well enough to do that. She'll be glad to do you a favor."

"That's true!" said Matilda, delighted. "I hadn't thought of that."

The next day she went to her friend's house and explained the situation. Mrs. Forester immediately opened a drawer, took out a large jewel box, and held it out to Matilda.

"Choose, my dear," she said.

Matilda saw some bracelets, a pearl necklace, and gold pins with jewels on them. She began **to try on** the jewelry in front of the mirror. Everything looked so beautiful it was hard to make up her mind.

Then suddenly she saw a magnificent diamond necklace. Her hands shook as she picked it up, and her heart pounded with desire as she held it against her neck. She looked at herself in delight.

She turned to Mrs. Forester. "Could—could you lend me this? Just this?" she gasped.

"Why, yes, certainly," said Mrs. Forester.

Matilda threw her arms around her friend and kissed her. Then she rushed home with her treasure.

The day of the party came. Mrs. Loisel was a great success. She was the prettiest woman there, charming and smiling. Everybody noticed her and admired her. Many men danced with her. The
90 Minister of Education himself asked who she was.

Matilda danced and danced, floating on a cloud of joy.

It was after midnight when they got ready to go home. "Wait here while I call a cab," said Mr. Loisel. "It's chilly outside. You might catch a cold."

95 But Matilda would not listen. She grabbed her old coat and rushed down the stairs. She did not want to be seen by the other women who were putting on their expensive furs.

After a few minutes they found a cab and headed for home. The cab stopped at their door and they **wearily** went up to their
100 apartment. Matilda kept thinking about the marvelous party. Then she realized, sadly, that the wonderful evening was over, all over. As for Mr. Loisel, he was thinking that he had to be at work by ten o'clock.

Matilda took off her coat in front of the mirror. She wanted to
105 take one last look at herself in her gown. Suddenly she cried out in horror, "The necklace! The diamond necklace! It's gone!"

Put an *x* in the box next to the correct answer.

Reading Comprehension

1. Matilda married
- ❏ **a.** the Minister of Education.
- ❏ **b.** a wealthy man.
- ❏ **c.** a clerk.

2. Matilda was unhappy because
- ❏ **a.** her health was bad.
- ❏ **b.** she had no friends.
- ❏ **c.** she did not have the things she wanted.

3. Matilda said she couldn't go to the party because she didn't
- ❏ **a.** know anyone there.
- ❏ **b.** own a good dress.
- ❏ **c.** want to stay up so late.

4. Mr. Loisel suggested that Matilda
- ❏ **a.** go to the party without jewels.
- ❏ **b.** earn money to buy jewels.
- ❏ **c.** borrow jewels from Mrs. Forester.

5. Mr. Loisel gave Matilda
- ❏ **a.** four hundred francs.
- ❏ **b.** five hundred francs.
- ❏ **c.** six hundred francs.

6. At the end of Part 1, Matilda was shocked because
- ❏ **a.** the necklace was gone.
- ❏ **b.** no one danced with her.
- ❏ **c.** her coat looked so old.

Vocabulary

7. Since Matilda's family was very poor, she could not meet a rich and distinguished man. The word *distinguished* means
- ❏ **a.** famous.
- ❏ **b.** strong.
- ❏ **c.** helpful.

8. She wondered how much money her thrifty husband would give her. People who are *thrifty*
- ❏ **a.** are very rich.
- ❏ **b.** don't care how much money they spend.
- ❏ **c.** try to save money by spending very carefully.

9. At the end of the day, they went wearily back to their apartment. The word *wearily* means
- ❏ **a.** very old.
- ❏ **b.** very tired.
- ❏ **c.** very smart.

Idioms

10. Matilda began to try on the jewelry. When you *try on* something, you
- ❏ **a.** buy it.
- ❏ **b.** lend it to someone.
- ❏ **c.** wear it to see if you like it.

How many questions did you answer correctly? Circle your score. Then fill in your score on the Score Chart on page 184.

Number Correct	1	2	3	4	5	6	7	8	9	10
Score	10	20	30	40	50	60	70	80	90	100

Exercise A

Understanding the story. Answer each question by writing a complete sentence. Begin each sentence with a capital letter, and end each sentence with a period. You may use the line numbers in parentheses to help you.

1. Whom did Matilda marry? (3)

    _____

2. What did Matilda dream of having? (6)

    _____

3. What did Matilda hate about the apartment she lived in? (16)

    _____

    _____

4. How did Matilda always feel when she returned from Jeanne's house? (20)

    _____

5. What did Matilda do with the invitation? (28)

    _____

6. What dress did Mr. Loisel expect his wife to wear to the party? (36)

    _____

7. How much did Matilda think a new gown would cost? (50)

    _____

8. What did Mrs. Forester lend Matilda? (79)

    _____

9. What time was it when they got ready to go home after the party? (92)

    _____

10. What did Matilda realize when she took off her coat? (106)

    _____

Exercise B

Part A

Putting events in order. Put the events in the order in which they occurred. You may look back at the story.

1. ____
2. ____
3. ____
4. ____
5. ____
6. ____
7. ____
8. ____

a. Mr. Loisel agreed to give Matilda money to buy a new gown.

b. The Loisels found a cab and went home.

c. Matilda threw the invitation on the table.

d. Matilda was upset because she didn't have any jewelry.

e. Mrs. Forester let Matilda borrow a diamond necklace.

f. Mr. Loisel gave Matilda an envelope.

g. Matilda said that the necklace was gone.

h. Many men danced with Matilda at the party.

Part B

Now list the correct order of the events on the lines below.

1. _____

2. _____

3. _____

   _____

4. _____

   _____

5. _____

6. _____

7. _____

8. _____

Exercise C

Adding vocabulary. On the left are 10 words from the story. Complete each sentence by adding the correct word.

gown

lid

luxuries

frowned

afford

rifle

magnificent

silverware

invitation

convince

1. Matilda wished that she had fine dresses and jewels and other _____ of life.

2. She did not have enough money to _____ a better apartment.

3. She dreamed of dinners served on beautiful plates with expensive _____.

4. At dinner, her husband would lift the _____ of a pot.

5. The little card was an _____ to a party at the Minister's house.

6. Instead of being happy and pleased, Matilda _____ at her husband.

7. She could not wear an old dress to the party; she needed a new _____.

8. He had saved money to buy a _____ to take on a hunting trip.

9. Although he explained that she could wear flowers, his words did not _____ her.

10. Matilda's heart began to pound when she saw the _____ necklace.

Exercise D

Using verbs correctly. Fill in the blanks in each sentence by writing the **future tense** of the verb in parentheses. Use *will* plus the verb. The first one has been done for you.

1. Mr. Loisel told Matilda, "Here is something you ___*will*___ ___*like*___." (like)

2. Many important people _____ _____ there. (be)

3. She said, "If I can buy a new gown, I _____ _____ to the party." (go)

4. A new gown _____ _____ about four hundred francs. (cost)

5. Mr. Loisel said, "I _____ _____ you the money." (give)

6. Matilda exclaimed, "Since I don't have any jewelry, I _____ _____ very poor!" (look)

7. He said, "She _____ _____ you some jewels." (lend)

8. Mr. Loisel told Matilda, "I _____ _____ a cab." (call)

9. Do you think they _____ _____ the necklace? (find)

10. What do you think they _____ _____ if they don't find the necklace? (do)

Write your own sentences in the **future tense** by using the verbs in parentheses.

11. (will try) _____

_____

12. (will speak) _____

_____

13. (will ask) _____

_____

14. (will return) _____

_____

15. (will borrow) _____

_____

Exercise E

Comparison of adjectives and adverbs. The following chart shows the comparison of some **adjectives** and **adverbs**. Use the chart to help you fill in the blanks in the sentences below. Use each word once. The first one has been done for you.

	Positive	Comparative	Superlative
	poor	poorer	poorest
	pretty	prettier	prettiest
	famous	more famous	most famous
(irregular)	good	better	best

1. Matilda had very little money. She was ___*poor*___.

2. Matilda did not have as much money as Mrs. Forester. Matilda was

   _____ than Mrs. Forester.

3. Everyone at the party had more money than Matilda. She was the

   _____ person there.

4. Matilda was very beautiful. She was the _____ woman there.

5. Last year's party was good, but this year's party was _____.

6. It was the _____ party anyone had ever been to.

7. The minister was very well known. He was the _____
   person at the party.

Write your own sentences using the words in parentheses.

8. (good) _____

   _____

9. (pretty) _____

   _____

10. (prettier) _____

    _____

11. (famous) _____

    _____

12. (more famous) _____

    _____

Exercise F

Vocabulary review. Write a complete sentence for each word or group of words.

1. invitation _____

_____

2. magnificent _____

_____

3. gown _____

_____

4. frowned _____

_____

5. luxuries _____

_____

6. convince _____

_____

7. distinguished _____

_____

8. thrifty _____

_____

9. wearily _____

_____

10. tried on _____

_____

SHARING WITH OTHERS

Everyone can learn by sharing ideas. Meet with your partner or group to discuss these questions. Write your answer to one of the questions.

◆ Suppose that Matilda didn't get the money to buy a new gown. Should she have gone to the party anyway? Explain your answer.

◆ As they returned to their apartment, Matilda was thinking about the wonderful party. Mr. Loisel was thinking that he had to be at work by ten o'clock. Suppose you are Matilda or Mr. Loisel. Write a paragraph that tells exactly what you are thinking.

_____

_____

_____

_____

_____

_____

_____

_____

_____

_____

_____

_____

PART 2

Matilda cried out in horror, "The necklace! The diamond necklace! It's gone!"

"What?" said Mr. Loisel. "That can't be! That's impossible!"

They looked in the folds of the gown, in the pockets of the coat.
5 They looked everywhere, but they could not find the necklace.

He asked, "Did you have it on when we left the party?"

"Yes, I felt it as we came down the stairs."

"But if you had lost it in the street, we would have heard it fall. It must be in the cab."

10 "Yes. Probably. Did you notice the cab number?"

"No. Did you?"

"No!" she answered.

They looked at each other, **horrified**. Finally Mr. Loisel said, "I'll go back over the route we took. Maybe I can find it somewhere."

15 He went out. Matilda walked to a chair, slumped down wearily in it, and waited in her evening gown. She did not have the strength to get up and go to bed. She was too **exhausted** to move or to think.

Mr. Loisel came back at seven o'clock. He had found nothing.

He went to the police and to the cab companies. He put an
20 advertisement in the newspapers, offering a reward. He did everything he could.

Meanwhile, Matilda waited all day, weak with fear. Her husband came back in the evening. His face was hollow and pale. He had discovered nothing.

25 "You must send a note to your friend," he said. "Thank her for lending you the necklace. Then say that you accidentally broke the lock on it and are having it repaired. That will give us more time."

She did as he said.

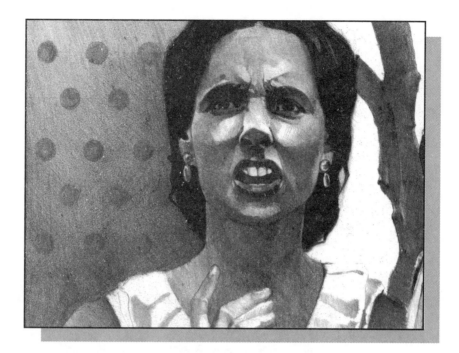

By the end of the week, they had lost all hope. Mr. Loisel, who
had aged by five years, shook his head and said, "We must find a
way to replace the necklace."

The next day they went from jeweler to jeweler, searching for a
necklace that looked like the one they had lost. At last, in a large
shop, they found a necklace that seemed just right. As far as they
could remember, it looked exactly like the other one. The jeweler
told them that it cost forty thousand francs, but he said that he was
willing to sell it to them for thirty-six thousand.

They begged the jeweler not to sell it for three days. Then they
thought about how to raise the money. Mr. Loisel's father had left
him a little. They would have to borrow the rest.

He borrowed it, borrowing a thousand francs here, five hundred
francs there. He signed notes and made deals. He agreed to pay high
rates of interest. He risked everything without knowing if he could
ever pay back the money. But finally he had it all—thirty-six
thousand francs. He brought the money to the jeweler and left the
shop with the diamond necklace.

Matilda took the necklace back to Mrs. Forester. Her friend said
coldly, "You should have returned this to me sooner. I might have
needed it."

Mrs. Forester hardly looked at the necklace. Matilda was
relieved. What if Jeanne had realized that it was a different necklace?
What would she have thought? What would she have said? Would
she have believed that Matilda was a thief?

From that day on, Matilda lived a life of poverty. She did not
complain, however. It was necessary to pay back that huge **debt**.
They would pay it.

They got rid of their housekeeper and moved to another
apartment, one that was cheaper. They saved money every way
they could. Matilda washed their clothing and did her own cooking.
Every day, dressed in old clothes, she went to the market where she
bargained and begged to save a few cents.

She got a job doing heavy housework. She washed laundry and
scrubbed floors and was busy from morning to night.

Her husband worked late every night. He checked orders for
some local merchants to earn a few extra francs.

Each month they paid back part of the money they owed.

Life went on like this for ten years.

At the end of ten years they had paid off the whole debt. Mrs.
Loisel looked old now. Her hair was messy and her hands were
rough and red. Her clothes were shabby, and she spoke in a loud,
shrill voice as she mopped the floors with big pails of water. But
once in a while, at the end of a long day, she sat looking out the
window. She thought about the wonderful party she went to long
ago. She remembered how beautiful she was and how everyone
admired her.

How would things have turned out if she had not lost that
necklace? Who knows? Who knows? Life is strange and full of twists.
One little thing can make all the difference.

One Sunday, after a very hard week, Matilda decided to take a
walk in the park. Suddenly she saw a woman walking with a child. It
was Jeanne Forester, still young, still pretty. Matilda wondered if she
should speak to her. Yes, certainly. Why not? And now that she had
paid the debt, she would tell her what happened.

Matilda approached her and said, "Good morning, Jeanne."

Her friend did not recognize her and was startled that a stranger
knew her first name. She said, "But—I do not know you. You must be
mistaken—"

"No, I am Matilda Loisel."

Her friend cried out, "Oh, Matilda! You look so different!"

"Yes, I have had some hard days since I saw you—some very
hard days. And all because of you—"

"Because of me? Why?"

"Do you remember the diamond necklace that you lent me
years ago?"

95 "Yes. What about it?"

"Well, I lost it."

"What do you mean? You returned it to me."

"I returned another one exactly like it. It has taken us ten years to pay for it. It was very difficult for us because my husband doesn't
100 make much money. But it's paid for now, and I'm glad that's over."

Mrs. Forester stared at Matilda and said very slowly, "You say that you bought a diamond necklace to replace mine?"

"Yes. You never noticed it, then! They were so alike." And Matilda smiled with a joy that was honest and proud.

105 Mrs. Forester was very moved. She gently took her friend's hands in her own as she spoke.

"Oh, my dear Matilda," she said. "My necklace was fake. It was made out of glass. It was not worth more than five hundred francs!"

YOU CAN ANSWER THESE QUESTIONS

Put an *x* in the box next to the correct answer.

Reading Comprehension

1. Matilda probably lost the necklace
   - ❑ **a.** on the way to the party.
   - ❑ **b.** while she was dancing.
   - ❑ **c.** in the cab.

2. Mr. Loisel asked Matilda to send a note to
   - ❑ **a.** the police.
   - ❑ **b.** Mrs. Forester.
   - ❑ **c.** the newspapers.

3. The jeweler was willing to sell them a necklace for
   - ❑ **a.** twenty-five thousand francs.
   - ❑ **b.** thirty thousand francs.
   - ❑ **c.** thirty-six thousand francs.

4. Mrs. Loisel earned money by
   - ❑ **a.** working late every night checking orders.
   - ❑ **b.** washing laundry and scrubbing floors.
   - ❑ **c.** working in a bank.

5. How long did it take to pay back the money they borrowed?
   - ❑ **a.** ten years
   - ❑ **b.** fifteen years
   - ❑ **c.** twenty years.

6. Mrs. Forester told Matilda that the necklace
   - ❑ **a.** cost a lot of money.
   - ❑ **b.** was not worth anything.
   - ❑ **c.** was made out of glass.

Vocabulary

7. Matilda was too exhausted to move or to think. The word *exhausted* means
   - ❑ **a.** tired.
   - ❑ **b.** happy.
   - ❑ **c.** brave.

8. They were horrified that the necklace was gone. The word *horrified* means
   - ❑ **a.** calm.
   - ❑ **b.** shocked.
   - ❑ **c.** foolish.

9. It took many years to pay back the debt. The word *debt* means
   - ❑ **a.** something you like.
   - ❑ **b.** something you owe.
   - ❑ **c.** something you need.

Idioms

10. Once in a while, Matilda thought about the party. The idiom *once in a while* means
    - ❑ **a.** sometimes.
    - ❑ **b.** very often.
    - ❑ **c.** never.

How many questions did you answer correctly? Circle your score. Then fill in your score on the Score Chart on page 184.

Number Correct	1	2	3	4	5	6	7	8	9	10
Score	10	20	30	40	50	60	70	80	90	100

Exercise A

Understanding the story. Answer each question by writing a complete sentence. Begin each sentence with a capital letter, and end each sentence with a period. You may use the line numbers in parentheses to help you.

1. How did they know that Matilda hadn't lost the necklace in the street? (8)

   _____

2. Where did Matilda probably lose the necklace? (9)

   _____

3. Why did they go from jeweler to jeweler? (32)

   _____

   _____

4. How much money did the jeweler want for the necklace? (37)

   _____

5. Why did the Loisels move to another apartment? (58)

   _____

6. How did Mr. Loisel earn a few extra francs? (64)

   _____

7. At the end of ten years, how did Mrs. Loisel look? (69)

   _____

8. What did Matilda think about once in a while? (73)

   _____

   _____

9. How did Jeanne Forester look? (81)

   _____

10. How much was Jeanne's necklace worth? (108)

   _____

Exercise B

Part A

Putting events in order. Put the events in the order in which they occurred. You may look back at the story.

1. ____
2. ____
3. ____
4. ____
5. ____
6. ____
7. ____
8. ____

a. Mr. Loisel borrowed money to pay for the necklace.

b. Matilda met Mrs. Forester in the park.

c. Matilda took the necklace to Mrs. Forester.

d. The Loisels looked in the pockets of the coat for the necklace.

e. The Loisels moved to a cheaper apartment.

f. Mr. Loisel went to the police and the cab companies.

g. Mrs. Forester said that the necklace was fake.

h. They found a necklace that looked like the one they had lost.

Part B

Now list the correct order of the events on the lines below.

1. _____

_____

2. _____

3. _____

_____

4. _____

5. _____

6. _____

7. _____

8. _____

Exercise C

Adding vocabulary. On the left are 10 words from the story. Complete each sentence by adding the correct word.

messy

route

accidentally

slumped

recognize

approached

replace

reward

repaired

poverty

1. Mr. Loisel went out to look for the necklace. He went back over the _____ they had taken.

2. Matilda was very tired; she _____ into a chair and waited for her husband.

3. Mr. Loisel offered a _____ to anyone who returned the necklace.

4. They said that the lock was broken and that they were having it _____.

5. The note said that they did not mean to break the lock; they broke it _____.

6. They went from jeweler to jeweler, looking for a necklace to _____ the one they had lost.

7. They lived in _____ because they were so poor.

8. Mrs. Loisel looked old; her hair was _____ and her hands were rough.

9. Matilda came close to Jeanne; Matilda _____ her.

10. At first Jeanne didn't know who Matilda was because Jeanne didn't _____ her.

Exercise D

Using verbs correctly. Fill in each blank using the **past tense** of the irregular verb in parentheses.

1. By the end of the week, they _____ all hope of finding the necklace. (lose)

2. Mr. Loisel _____ his head sadly. (shake)

3. In a large shop they _____ a necklace that seemed just right. (find)

4. They _____ about how to pay for the necklace. (think)

5. After three days, he _____ all the money he needed. (have)

6. Mr. Loisel _____ the money to the jeweler and left with the necklace. (bring)

7. Matilda _____ the necklace back to Mrs. Forester. (take)

8. Mrs. Forester said, "You should have returned this sooner. I

   _____ have needed it." (may)

9. Matilda washed their clothing and _____ her own cooking. (do)

10. She _____ a job doing heavy housework. (get)

11. Mrs. Loisel _____ in a loud voice. (speak)

12. Sometimes she _____ looking out of the window. (sit)

13. Suddenly Matilda _____ a woman walking with a child. (see)

14. Jeanne was surprised that a stranger _____ her name. (know)

15. She was shocked to hear that Matilda _____ another necklace. (buy)

Exercise E

Picking a preposition. Fill in each blank by adding the correct **preposition**. Use each preposition once.

with	until	about	in
down	from	for	at

1. Matilda felt the necklace as she walked _____ the stairs.

2. They did not lose the necklace _____ the street.

3. The next day they went _____ jeweler to jeweler.

4. They were searching _____ a new necklace.

5. Mrs. Forester hardly looked _____ the necklace.

6. Mr. Loisel worked every night _____ it got dark.

7. Sometimes Matilda thought _____ the Minister's party.

8. Matilda saw Mrs. Forester walking _____ a child.

Write your own sentences using the prepositions in parentheses.

9. (into) _____

_____

10. (on) _____

_____

11. (across) _____

_____

12. (over) _____

_____

13. (below) _____

_____

14. (up) _____

_____

15. (under) _____

_____

Exercise F

Vocabulary review. Write a complete sentence for each word or group of words.

1. reward _____

_____

2. poverty _____

_____

3. recognize _____

_____

4. approached _____

_____

5. repaired _____

_____

6. accidentally _____

_____

7. exhausted _____

_____

8. horrified _____

_____

9. debt _____

_____

10. once in a while _____

_____

SHARING WITH OTHERS

Everyone can learn by sharing ideas. Meet with your partner or group to discuss these questions. Write your answer to one of the questions.

◆ If you were Matilda, would you have written a letter to your friend saying that you were having the necklace repaired? Would you have told Jeanne the truth? Would you have done something else? Explain your answer.

◆ Now that Mrs. Forester knows that the necklace is valuable, should she return it to the Loisels? Should she pay them for it? Is it really possible to pay back the Loisels? Give reasons for your answers.

_____

_____

_____

_____

_____

_____

_____

_____

_____

_____

_____

_____

_____

_____

KADDO'S
WALL

A West African Folktale

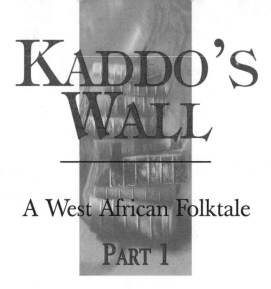

KADDO'S WALL

A West African Folktale

PART 1

"Kaddo's Wall" is a West African story. The people of Ghana appear in many West African folktales.

In the town of Tendella in the Kingdom of Seno, north of the Gulf of Guinea, there was a rich man by the name of Kaddo. His fields spread out on every side of the town. At plowing time[1] hundreds of men and boys hoed up his fields, and then hundreds of women and
5 girls planted his corn seed in the ground for him. His grain **bulged** in his granary[2] because each season he harvested far more than he could use.

The name of Kaddo was known far and wide throughout the Kingdom of Seno. Travelers who passed through the town carried
10 tales of his wealth far beyond Seno's borders.

One day Kaddo called all of his people in the town of Tendella together for a big meeting in front of his house. They all came, for Kaddo was an important man, and they knew he was going to make an important announcement.

15 "There's something that bothers me," Kaddo said. "I've been thinking about it for a long time. I've lain awake worrying. I have so much corn in my granary that I don't know what to do with it."

The people listened **attentively** and thought about Kaddo's words. Then a man said, "Some of the people of the town have no
20 corn at all. They are very poor and have nothing. Why don't you give some of your corn to them?"

Kaddo shook his head and said, "No, that isn't a very good idea. It doesn't satisfy me."

1. *plowing time:* the time of year when the earth is broken up (plowed or hoed) so that seeds can be planted.
2. *granary:* a building where grain (wheat, corn, oats, etc.) is kept.

Another man said to Kaddo, "Well, then, you could lend corn to the people who have had a bad harvest and have no seed for the spring planting. That would be very good for the town and would keep poverty away."

"No," Kaddo said, "that's no solution either."

"Well, then, why not sell some of your corn and buy cattle instead?" still another man said.

Kaddo shook his head.

"No, it's not very good advice. It's hard for people to advise a rich man with problems like mine."

Many people made suggestions, but nobody's advice suited Kaddo. He thought for a while, and at last he said, "Send me as many young girls as you can find. I will have them grind the corn for me."

The people went away. They were angry with Kaddo. But the next day they sent a hundred girls to work for him as he had asked. On a hundred grindstones[3] they began to grind Kaddo's corn into flour. All day long they put corn into the grindstones and took flour out. **All day** long the people of the town heard the sound of the grinding at Kaddo's house. A pile of corn flour began to grow. For seven days and seven nights the girls ground corn without a pause.

When the last grain of corn was ground into flour, Kaddo called the girls together and said, "Now bring water from the spring. We

3. *grindstone:* a hard, round stone used for grinding corn.

shall mix it with the corn flour to make mortar[4] out of it."

So the girls brought water in water pots and mixed it with the flour to make a thick mortar. Then Kaddo ordered them to make bricks out of the mortar.

"When the bricks are dry, then I shall make a wall of them around my house," he said.

Word went out that Kaddo was preparing to build a wall of flour around his house, and the people of the town came to his door and protested.

"You can't do a thing like this. It is against humanity!"[5] they said.

"It's not right; people have no right to build walls with *food*!" a man said.

"Ah, what is right and what is wrong?" Kaddo said. "My right is different from yours because I am so very rich. So **leave me alone**."

"Corn is to eat so that you may keep alive," another said. "It's not meant to taunt those who are less fortunate."

"When people are hungry it is an affront[6] to shut them out with a wall of flour," another man said.

"Stop your complaints," Kaddo said. "The corn is mine. It is my surplus. I can't eat it all. It comes from my own fields. I am rich. What good is it to be rich if you can't do what you want with your own property?"

The people of the town went away, shaking their heads in anger over Kaddo's madness. The hundred girls continued to make bricks of flour, which they dried in the sun. And when the bricks were dry Kaddo had them begin building the wall around his house. They used wet dough for mortar to hold the bricks together, and slowly the wall grew. They stuck cowry shells[7] into the wall to make beautiful designs, and when at last the wall was done, and the last corn flour used up, Kaddo was very proud. He walked back and forth and looked at his wall. He walked around it. He went in and out of the gate. He was very happy.

4. *mortar:* something used for holding bricks or stones together.

5. *humanity:* human beings; people everywhere.

6. *affront:* something terrible that is said or done to another person.

7. *cowry shells:* shells that are smooth and have very bright colors.

And now when people came to see him they had to stand by the
gate until he asked them to enter. When the workers who plowed
and planted for Kaddo wanted to talk to him, Kaddo sat on the wall
by the gate and listened to them and gave them orders. And
whenever the people of the town wanted his opinion on an
important matter, he sat on his wall and gave it to them, while they
stood and listened.

Things went on like this for a long time. Kaddo enjoyed his
reputation as the richest man for miles around. The story of Kaddo's
wall went to the farthest parts of the kingdom.

Put an *x* in the box next to the correct answer.

Reading Comprehension

1. Kaddo didn't know what to do because he
   - ❑ **a.** didn't have enough corn.
   - ❑ **b.** had too much corn.
   - ❑ **c.** didn't like to eat corn.

2. A man suggested that Kaddo give some of his corn to
   - ❑ **a.** Kaddo's friends.
   - ❑ **b.** everyone in town.
   - ❑ **c.** people who were poor.

3. Someone suggested that Kaddo
   - ❑ **a.** sell some of his corn for cattle.
   - ❑ **b.** fill his house with corn.
   - ❑ **c.** take some of his corn to the next village.

4. Kaddo finally decided to
   - ❑ **a.** fill his garden with flour.
   - ❑ **b.** build a house of flour.
   - ❑ **c.** build a wall of flour.

5. When the people heard what Kaddo was planning to do, they
   - ❑ **a.** were glad.
   - ❑ **b.** were angry.
   - ❑ **c.** were quiet.

6. Kaddo often
   - ❑ **a.** sat on the wall and spoke to the people.
   - ❑ **b.** worked in his fields.
   - ❑ **c.** did what the people said.

Vocabulary

7. Kaddo had so much grain that it bulged in his granary. The word *bulged* means
   - ❑ **a.** stuck out of.
   - ❑ **b.** was empty.
   - ❑ **c.** was hard to see.

8. They listened attentively and thought about his words. The word *attentively* means
   - ❑ **a.** cheerfully.
   - ❑ **b.** sadly.
   - ❑ **c.** closely and carefully.

Idioms

9. The people heard the sound of the grindstones all day. The idiom *all day* means
   - ❑ **a.** for a few minutes.
   - ❑ **b.** an hour or two.
   - ❑ **c.** the whole day.

10. Kaddo did not like what the people said. He told them, "Leave me alone." The idiom *leave me alone* means
   - ❑ **a.** tell me more.
   - ❑ **b.** stay away from me.
   - ❑ **c.** I agree with you.

How many questions did you answer correctly? Circle your score. Then fill in your score on the Score Chart on page 184.

Number Correct	1	2	3	4	5	6	7	8	9	10
Score	10	20	30	40	50	60	70	80	90	100

Exercise A

Understanding the story. Answer each question by writing a complete sentence. Begin each sentence with a capital letter, and end each sentence with a period. You may use the line numbers in parentheses to help you.

1. Where did Kaddo live? (1)

2. How many men and boys hoed Kaddo's fields? (3)

3. How many women and girls planted Kaddo's corn? (4)

4. Where was the big meeting going to be? (12)

5. What was worrying Kaddo? (16)

6. What did a man suggest Kaddo do with some of his corn? (20)

7. For how many days and nights did the girls grind corn? (44)

8. What was Kaddo preparing to build around his house? (53)

9. What did they stick into the wall? (74)

10. Where did Kaddo sit when the workers wanted to talk to him? (81)

Exercise B

Part A

Putting events in order. Put the events in the order in which they occurred. You may look back at the story.

1. ____

2. ____

3. ____

4. ____

5. ____

6. ____

7. ____

a. Kaddo said that he didn't know what to do with his corn.

b. The people were angry with Kaddo for building a wall with food.

c. Kaddo called the people of the town to a big meeting.

d. Kaddo sat on his wall and gave orders.

e. Kaddo didn't like the advice he received.

f. People gave Kaddo some advice at the meeting.

g. The people heard that Kaddo was going to build a wall made of flour.

Part B

Now list the correct order of the events on the lines below.

1. _____

_____

2. _____

_____

3. _____

4. _____

5. _____

_____

6. _____

_____

7. _____

Exercise C

Adding vocabulary. On the left are 10 words from the story. Complete each sentence by adding the correct word.

pause

solution

fortunate

announcement

designs

harvested

opinion

surplus

protested

taunt

1. Kaddo was going to speak to the people. He was going to make an _____.

2. Each season Kaddo gathered a large amount of grain. He _____ more grain than he needed.

3. Kaddo did not agree with the answer they gave him. He did not think it was the _____ to the problem.

4. They ground the corn without stopping once. They ground the corn without a _____.

5. The people did not like what Kaddo was doing. They came to his door and _____.

6. Kaddo had more corn than he could use. He had a _____.

7. It was wrong of Kaddo to make fun of people. It was wrong of him to _____ them.

8. Some people are lucky. Others are not so _____.

9. They built the wall using bright, smooth shells. The shells made beautiful _____ on the wall.

10. Sometimes the people wanted to know what Kaddo thought. Then they asked him for his _____.

Exercise D

Part A

Using verbs correctly. Fill in the blanks using the **present tense** of the verb in parentheses. The first one has been done for you.

1. A rich man named Kaddo ___*owns*___ many fields of corn. (own)

2. Kaddo _____ many people working in his fields. (have)

3. Hundreds of workers plow his land and then _____ corn. (plant)

4. Travelers who pass through the town _____ tales of his wealth to other lands. (carry)

5. One day Kaddo _____ all the people in the town to a big meeting. (call)

6. Everybody _____ carefully to Kaddo. (listen)

7. Kaddo _____ the people what he should do with all the corn he has. (ask)

8. Several people _____ Kaddo advice. (give)

9. However, Kaddo _____ that he doesn't like their advice. (say)

10. He _____ to build a wall of flour around his house. (decide)

Part B

Summarize this part of the story by writing the sentences on the lines below. Use sentences 1–4 in your first paragraph. Use sentences 5–10 in your second paragraph. Remember to indent the second paragraph. The first sentence has been done for you.

A rich man named Kaddo owns many fields of corn.

_____

_____

_____

_____

_____

_____

_____

_____

_____

_____

_____

_____

_____

Exercise E

Putting words in correct order. Unscramble each sentence by putting the words in the correct order. Write each sentence on the line. Each sentence is in the **past tense**.

1. men / of / fields / Kaddo's / hoed / Hundreds

_____.

2. corn / the / ground / hundred / A / girls

_____.

3. beautiful / They / into / put / wall / shells / the

_____

_____.

4. proud / was / his / of / wall / very / Kaddo

_____.

5. on / sit / He / to / liked / wall / his

_____.

6. The / listened / workers / orders / to / Kaddo's

_____.

7. told / wall / Kaddo's / of / Everyone / story / the

_____

_____.

Now look at the sentences you wrote. Underline the verb in the **past tense** in each sentence.

Exercise F

Vocabulary review. Write a complete sentence for each word or group of words.

1. announcement _____

_____

2. fortunate _____

_____

3. opinion _____

_____

4. harvested _____

_____

5. pause _____

_____

6. taunt _____

_____

7. surplus _____

_____

8. protested _____

_____

9. attentively _____

_____

10. all day _____

_____

Everyone can learn by sharing ideas. Meet with your partner or group to discuss these questions. Write your answer to one of the questions.

◆ Kaddo told a man who was poor, "What is right and what is wrong? My right is different from yours because I am so very rich." What did Kaddo mean by this? Do you agree with Kaddo? Why?

◆ How do you think the story will end? In a paragraph summarize what you think will happen.

_____

_____

_____

_____

_____

_____

_____

_____

_____

_____

_____

_____

_____

_____

_____

PART 2

And then one year there was a bad harvest for Kaddo. There wasn't enough rain to grow the corn, and the earth dried up hard and dusty like the road. There wasn't a single ear of corn in all of Kaddo's fields or the fields of his relatives.

5   The next year it was the same. Kaddo had no seed corn left, so he sold his cattle and horses to buy corn for food and seed for a new planting. He sowed corn again, but the next harvest time it was the same, and there wasn't a single ear of corn on all his fields.

Year after year Kaddo's crops failed. Some of his relatives died of 10   hunger, and others went away to other parts of the Kingdom of Seno, for they had no more seed corn to plant and they couldn't **count on** Kaddo's help. Kaddo's workers ran away, because he was unable to feed them. Gradually Kaddo's part of the town became **deserted**. All that he had left were a young daughter and a mangy[1] donkey.

15   When his cattle and his money were all gone, Kaddo became very hungry. He scraped away a little bit of the flour wall and ate it. Next day he scraped away more of the flour wall and ate it. The wall got lower and lower. **Little by little** it disappeared. A day came when the wall was gone, when nothing was left of the elegant 20   structure[2] Kaddo had built around his house, and on which he had used to sit to listen to the people of the town when they came to ask him to lend them a little seed corn.

Then Kaddo realized that if he was to live any longer he must get help from somewhere. He wondered who would help him. Not the 25   people of Tendella, for he had insulted and mistreated[3] them and they would have nothing to do with him. There was only one man

1. *mangy:* worn-out and dirty.
2. *elegant structure:* something that has been built very beautifully.
3. *mistreated:* treated badly; acted badly to.

he could go to, Sogole, king of the Ghana people, who had the
reputation of being very rich and generous.

So Kaddo and his daughter got on the mangy, underfed donkey
and rode seven days until they arrived in the land of the Ghana.

Sogole sat before his royal house when Kaddo arrived. He had a
soft skin put on the ground next to him for Kaddo to sit upon, and
had millet beer brought for the two of them to drink.

"Well, stranger in the land of the Ghana, take a long drink, for
you have a long trip behind you if you came from Tendella,"
Sogole said.

"Thank you, but I can't drink too much," Kaddo said.

"Why is that?" Sogole said. "When people are thirsty they drink."

"That is true," Kaddo replied. "But I have been hungry too long,
and my stomach has shrunk."

"Well, drink in peace then, because now that you are my guest
you won't be hungry. You shall have whatever you need from me."

Kaddo nodded his head solemnly[4] and drank a little of the millet
beer.

"And now tell me," Sogole said. "You say you come from the
town of Tendella in the Kingdom of Seno? I've heard many tales of
that town. The **famine** came there and drove out many people
because they had no corn left."

"Yes," Kaddo said. "Hard times drove them out, and the corn
was all gone."

"But tell me, there was a rich and powerful man in Tendella

4. *solemnly:* very seriously.

named Kaddo, wasn't there? Whatever happened to him? Is he still alive?"

"Yes, he is still alive," Kaddo said.

"A fabulous[5] man, this Kaddo," Sogole said. "They say he built a wall of flour around his house out of his surplus crops, and when he talked to his people he sat on the wall by his gate. Is this true?"

"Yes, it is true," Kaddo said sadly.

"Does he still have as many cattle as he used to?" Sogole asked.

"No, they are all gone."

"It is an unhappy thing for a man who owned so much to come to so little," Sogole said. "But doesn't he have many servants and workers still?"

"His workers and servants are all gone," Kaddo said. "Of all his great household he has only one daughter left. The rest went away because there was no money and no food."

Sogole looked melancholy.[6]

"Ah, what is a rich man when his cattle are gone and his servants have left him? But tell me, what happened to the wall of flour that he built around his house?"

"He ate the wall," Kaddo said. "Each day he scraped a little of the flour from the wall, until it was all gone."

"A strange story," Sogole said. "But such is life."

And he thought quietly for a while about the way life goes for people sometimes, and then he asked, "And were you, by any chance, one of Kaddo's family?"

"Indeed I was one of Kaddo's family. Once I was rich. Once I had more cattle than I could count. Once I had many cornfields. Once I had hundreds of workers cultivating[7] my crops. Once I had a bursting granary. Once I was Kaddo, the great man of Tendella."

"What! You yourself are Kaddo?"

"Yes, once I was proud and lordly,[8] and now I sit in rags begging for help."

"What can I do for you?" Sogole asked.

"I have nothing left now. Give me some seed corn, so that I can go back and plant my fields again."

5. *fabulous:* As used here, the word means "very unusual or amazing."

6. *melancholy:* very sad.

7. *cultivating:* As used here, the word means "preparing and working on crops."

8. *lordly:* like a king or a lord.

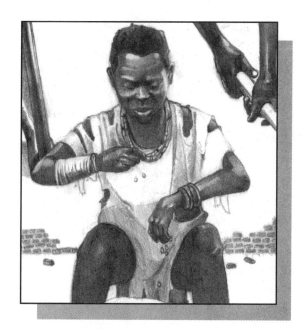

"Take what you need," Sogole said. He ordered his servants to bring bags of corn and to load them on Kaddo's donkey. Kaddo thanked him humbly, and he and his daughter started their return
90 trip to Tendella.

They traveled for seven days. On the way Kaddo became very hungry. He hadn't seen so much corn for a long time as he was bringing back from the Kingdom of the Ghana. He took a few grains and put them in his mouth and chewed them. Once more he put a
95 few grains in his mouth. Then he put a whole handful in his mouth and swallowed. He couldn't stop. He ate and ate. He forgot that this was the corn with which he had to plant his fields. When he arrived in Tendella he went to his bed to sleep, and when he arose the next morning he ate again. He ate so much of the corn that he became
100 sick. He went to his bed again and cried out in pain, because his stomach had forgotten what to do with food. And before long Kaddo died.

Kaddo's grandchildren and great-grandchildren in the Kingdom of Seno are poor to this day. And to the rich men of the country the
105 common people sometimes say, "Don't build a wall of flour around your house!"

Put an *x* in the box next to the correct answer.

Reading Comprehension

1. Kaddo sold his cattle and horses to buy
   - ❏ **a.** corn and seed.
   - ❏ **b.** bread.
   - ❏ **c.** a donkey.

2. When Kaddo's money was gone, he began to
   - ❏ **a.** beg for food.
   - ❏ **b.** look for work.
   - ❏ **c.** eat the flour wall.

3. Kaddo got help from
   - ❏ **a.** his workers.
   - ❏ **b.** the people of Tendella.
   - ❏ **c.** Sogole.

4. Which statement is true?
   - ❏ **a.** Sogole was not rich.
   - ❏ **b.** Sogole had heard about a man named Kaddo.
   - ❏ **c.** Sogole had not heard about Kaddo.

5. Sogole gave Kaddo
   - ❏ **a.** some cows.
   - ❏ **b.** bags of corn.
   - ❏ **c.** a little bit of flour.

6. Kaddo became sick because he
   - ❏ **a.** drank too much.
   - ❏ **b.** ate too much.
   - ❏ **c.** didn't get enough sleep.

Vocabulary

7. Everyone left the town, and soon it was deserted. The word *deserted* means
   - ❏ **a.** busy.
   - ❏ **b.** noisy.
   - ❏ **c.** empty.

8. When the corn was gone, many people died of famine. There is *famine* when
   - ❏ **a.** it is hard to find a job.
   - ❏ **b.** food costs a lot.
   - ❏ **c.** there is no food.

Idioms

9. People left Kaddo. They couldn't count on him. When you *count on* someone, you
   - ❏ **a.** know that the person will help you.
   - ❏ **b.** know how old the person is.
   - ❏ **c.** can count how much money the person has.

10. Little by little the wall got smaller. When something happens *little by little*, it happens
    - ❏ **a.** slowly.
    - ❏ **b.** quickly.
    - ❏ **c.** happily.

How many questions did you answer correctly? Circle your score. Then fill in your score on the Score Chart on page 184.

Number Correct	1	2	3	4	5	6	7	8	9	10
Score	10	20	30	40	50	60	70	80	90	100

Exercise A

Understanding the story. Answer each question by writing a complete sentence. Begin each sentence with a capital letter, and end each sentence with a period. You may use the line numbers in parentheses to help you.

1. Why did Kaddo sell his cattle and horses? (6)

   _____

2. Why did Kaddo's workers run away? (12)

   _____

3. What did Kaddo do when his money was gone and he was hungry? (16)

   _____

4. To whom did Kaddo decide to go for help? (27)

   _____

5. How long did Kaddo and his daughter ride until they arrived in the land of the Ghana? (30)

   _____

6. Why did everyone except Kaddo's daughter go away? (65)

   _____

   _____

7. What did Kaddo ask Sogole to give him? (85)

   _____

8. What did Kaddo forget? (96)

   _____

   _____

9. Why did Kaddo cry out in pain? (100)

   _____

10. What do the common people sometimes say to the rich men of the country? (105)

    _____

    _____

Exercise B

Part A

Putting events in order. Put the events in the order in which they occurred. You may look back at the story.

1. ____
2. ____
3. ____
4. ____
5. ____
6. ____
7. ____

a. Sogole asked his visitor about a man named Kaddo.

b. Kaddo's corn did not grow.

c. Kaddo began to eat his flour wall.

d. Kaddo died.

e. Kaddo couldn't stop eating the corn.

f. Sogole gave Kaddo some bags of corn.

g. Kaddo asked Sogole for some seed corn.

h. Kaddo and his daughter went to the land of the Ghana.

Part B

Now list the correct order of the events on the lines below.

1. _____

2. _____

3. _____

_____

4. _____

_____

5. _____

6. _____

7. _____

8. _____

Exercise C

Adding vocabulary. On the left are 10 words from the story. Complete each sentence by adding the correct word.

generous

relatives

disappeared

sowed

rags

stomach

scraped

insulted

swallowed

humbly

1. Kaddo _____ seeds in his fields, but the corn did not grow.

2. All of Kaddo's _____ except his daughter went away.

3. Each day Kaddo _____ away a little bit of the wall and ate it.

4. One day the wall was gone; it had _____.

5. Kaddo knew that the people of Tendella wouldn't help him because he had _____ them.

6. Sogole was willing to give Kaddo whatever he wanted; Sogole was _____.

7. Kaddo once had beautiful clothes, but now he was dressed in _____.

8. Kaddo was grateful to Sogole and thanked him _____.

9. Kaddo put a mouthful of corn in his mouth and _____.

10. Kaddo had been hungry for so long that his _____ had shrunk.

Exercise D

Using verbs correctly. Below are five forms of the verb *to go*. Fill in the blanks by writing the correct form of the verb. Use each word once.

go   goes   going   went   gone

1. Kaddo told his daughter, "We must _____ to the land of the Ghana."

2. Kaddo said that all of his workers had _____ away.

3. While he was _____ home, Kaddo kept eating the corn.

4. When he returned to Tendella, Kaddo felt sick and

   _____ to bed.

5. Almost every day, Sogole _____ into town and speaks to the people.

Below are five forms of the verb *to give*. Fill in the blanks by writing the correct form of the verb. Use each word once.

give   gives   giving   gave   given

6. Kaddo said, "Please _____ me some corn so that I can plant my fields."

7. Sogole _____ Kaddo some large bags of corn.

8. Kaddo thanked Sogole for _____ him the corn.

9. Kaddo ate all the corn that Sogole had _____ him.

10. Whenever anyone asks Sogole for food, he _____ the person something to eat.

Exercise E

Adding punctuation. The following passage needs **punctuation marks**. Add capital letters, periods, question marks, commas, and quotation marks. Then write the corrected passage on the lines below.

kaddo became a poor man his corn cattle cows servants and money were gone then he and his daughter traveled to ghana there they met sogole kaddo told sogole that he came from the town of tendella in seno sogole asked kaddo wasn't there a rich man named kaddo in tendella what happened to him is he still alive

_____

_____

_____

_____

_____

_____

_____

_____

_____

_____

_____

_____

_____

Exercise F

Vocabulary review. Write a complete sentence for each word or group of words.

1. disappeared _____

   _____

2. generous _____

   _____

3. rags _____

   _____

4. insulted _____

   _____

5. swallowed _____

   _____

6. relatives _____

   _____

7. deserted _____

   _____

8. famine _____

   _____

9. little by little _____

   _____

10. count on _____

   _____

SHARING WITH OTHERS

Everyone can learn by sharing ideas. Meet with your partner or group to discuss these questions. Write your answer to one of the questions.

◆ Compare Kaddo and Sogole. In what ways were they alike? How were they different?

◆ The story ends with a moral, or lesson: "Don't build a wall of flour around your house." What do these words mean?

_____

_____

_____

_____

_____

_____

_____

_____

_____

_____

_____

_____

_____

_____

THE
COMEBACK

by Elizabeth Van Steenwyk

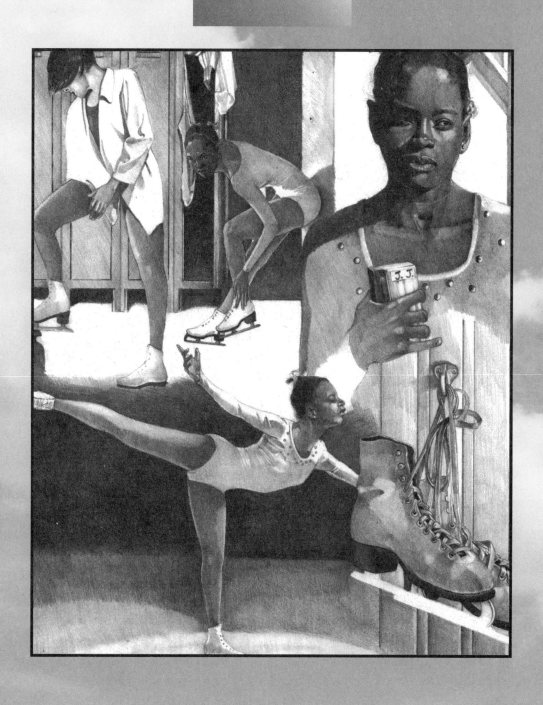

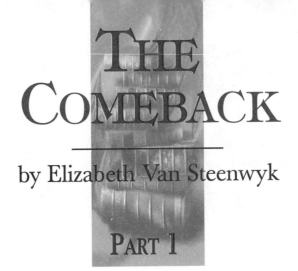

THE COMEBACK

by Elizabeth Van Steenwyk

PART 1

In this story, a young skater returns to the ice after a serious accident. Will she be successful in her comeback?

Laurie sat quietly in the empty dressing room at the ice-skating rink. She had not skated in competition since the accident six months ago. As she waited for her turn to skate, Laurie was very nervous. She knew that today was a very important day in her comeback.

5   "*If* I can win today," she thought, "I can skate in the World Cup next year. *If* I do well there, maybe I can make it to the Olympics. That would be **fantastic**!"

Before Laurie had her accident, no one could beat her in competition. From the day when she was ten and started to compete,
10   she had beaten all her opponents.

"Hello, Laurie," Kathy said, suddenly bursting through the door. "Welcome back to competition! We've missed you these last six months."

"I've missed being here," Laurie said.

15   "How's the knee?" Kathy asked, looking serious. "Is it going to slow you down? I mean you were skating so well before you got hurt. We really thought you'd be in the Seniors by now and then in the Olympics."

"I guess we'll find out tonight just where I stand," Laurie said.

20   "We have some new competition this year," Kathy said, tying her laces. "There's a girl from Connecticut named Jinny Jordan who's really strong in everything."

"I saw her skating this morning," Laurie said. "She was unbelievable!"

"Wait until you see her program tonight," Kathy said. "She does four
25   double axels and a triple toe loop[1] at the end. Can you believe it?"

1. *four double axels and a triple toe loop:* very hard jumps on the ice.

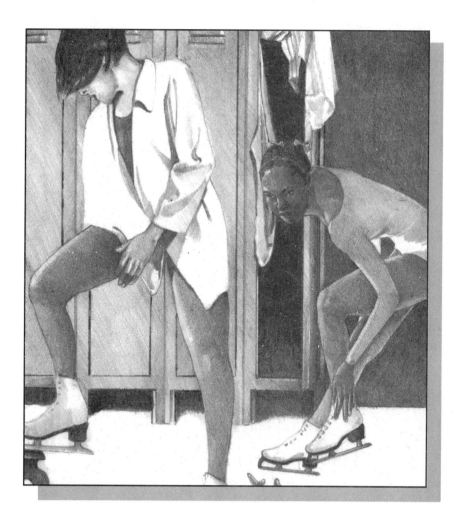

Laurie thought about this and knew that she would have to do a triple toe loop too. She had hoped to leave it out of her program because it put an added strain on her knee. But now there was no choice. "I'll just have to try the triple and hope for the best," she

30 thought. "If I don't try it, I won't **stand a chance**."

"Is Jinny ahead in the scoring?" Laurie asked.

"She's the one you have to beat this year," Kathy replied as she hurried out, slamming the door behind her.

For a moment Laurie sat quietly, getting used to the feeling of

35 being back. Until the accident, everyone had said that she was the one to beat. Now the one she had to beat was Jinny Jordan—someone she'd never heard of before. "Does anyone believe that I can still win?" she wondered. "Has everyone **given up** on me since the accident?"

40 The accident. Who could have predicted it? She thought back to that awful, rainy night when she and Mom were driving home after a practice session. The car in front of them **swerved** on the slippery road and they smashed into it. Later, examinations at the hospital showed that she had **damaged** her right knee badly. She would

need three months to heal and three more months of treatment and practice if she hoped to regain her skill.

Laurie suddenly jumped up as her right knee sent pain up and down her leg. The doctor said it would do that for a while. She waited for the pain to pass. Then she moved slowly across the room and back to warm up. She did a few knee bends, holding on to the top of the chair for support.

Suddenly she stood straight up and said to herself, "Who are you kidding! What makes you think you have a chance tonight?"

Then she said firmly, "I just *have* to win!"

The door swung open and Laurie saw a young woman who was about her own age but shorter and more powerfully built. At the moment her arms were filled with a skate equipment bag, a warm-up jacket, and a pair of skates.

The young woman dumped some of her belongings onto a chair. The bag fell to the floor with a thud. "Hi, I'm Jinny Jordan," she said.

Put an *x* in the box next to the correct answer.

Reading Comprehension

1. Laurie had been in an accident
- ❏ **a.** two months ago.
- ❏ **b.** six months ago.
- ❏ **c.** a year ago.

2. From the day when she was ten, Laurie had
- ❏ **a.** lost to some of the other skaters.
- ❏ **b.** lost to most of the other skaters.
- ❏ **c.** beaten all the other skaters.

3. Laurie was hoping that she wouldn't have to
- ❏ **a.** do a triple toe loop.
- ❏ **b.** skate very fast.
- ❏ **c.** be the last person to skate.

4. The doctor said that Laurie
- ❏ **a.** would have pain in her knee for a while.
- ❏ **b.** would not have any more pain in her knee.
- ❏ **c.** would not be able to skate again.

5. Jinny was the same age as Laurie, but Jinny was
- ❏ **a.** taller.
- ❏ **b.** shorter.
- ❏ **c.** weaker.

Vocabulary

6. It would be fantastic if Laurie could skate in the Olympics. The word *fantastic* means
- ❏ **a.** very good.
- ❏ **b.** very tired.
- ❏ **c.** very long.

7. A car swerved on the wet road and they smashed into it. The word *swerved* means
- ❏ **a.** got lost.
- ❏ **b.** turned suddenly.
- ❏ **c.** went faster.

8. Laurie had damaged her knee badly. The word *damaged* means
- ❏ **a.** hurt.
- ❏ **b.** needed.
- ❏ **c.** fixed.

Idioms

9. If Laurie didn't try a hard jump, she didn't stand a chance. The idiom *to stand a chance* means
- ❏ **a.** to stand still.
- ❏ **b.** to stand near.
- ❏ **c.** to have a chance.

10. Laurie wondered if everyone had given up on her. When you *give up,* you
- ❏ **a.** try very hard.
- ❏ **b.** think you will win.
- ❏ **c.** think you will lose.

How many questions did you answer correctly? Circle your score. Then fill in your score on the Score Chart on page 184.

Number Correct	1	2	3	4	5	6	7	8	9	10
Score	10	20	30	40	50	60	70	80	90	100

Exercise A

Understanding the story. Answer each question by writing a complete sentence. Begin each sentence with a capital letter, and end each sentence with a period. You may use the line numbers in parentheses to help you.

1. Where was Laurie sitting? (1)

_____

2. When did Laurie have an accident? (2)

_____

3. As Laurie waited to skate, how did she feel? (3)

_____

4. Who could beat Laurie before she had her accident? (8)

_____

5. Where was Jinny Jordan from? (21)

_____

6. What did Laurie want to leave out of her program? (27)

_____

7. Who was the one Laurie had to beat? (32)

_____

8. What kind of night was it when the accident took place? (41)

_____

9. Why did Laurie suddenly jump up? (47)

_____

_____

10. What was Jinny holding in her arms? (57)

_____

_____

Exercise B

Part A

Putting events in order. Put the events in the order in which they occurred. You may look back at the story.

1. ____

2. ____

3. ____

4. ____

5. ____

6. ____

7. ____

a. Kathy suddenly burst through the door.

b. A young woman said, "Hi, I'm Jinny Jordan."

c. Laurie realized that she would have to try a triple toe loop.

d. Kathy welcomed Laurie back to competition.

e. Laurie thought about the rainy night when she was in the accident.

f. Laurie sat quietly in the dressing room and thought about her comeback.

g. Kathy told Laurie about Jinny Jordan.

Part B

Now list the correct order of the events on the lines below.

1. _____

_____

2. _____

3. _____

4. _____

5. _____

_____

6. _____

_____

7. _____

Exercise C

Adding vocabulary. On the left are 10 words from the story. Complete each sentence by adding the correct word.

laces

slippery

compete

opponents

thud

examinations

heal

predicted

strain

support

1. Laurie had always beaten all her _____.

2. She was only ten years old when she started to _____.

3. Laurie tied the _____ on her skates.

4. Doing very hard jumps put a _____ on Laurie's knee.

5. Who would have guessed that Laurie would have an accident? Who could have _____ it?

6. It was a rainy night and the road was _____.

7. Later, _____ at the hospital showed that Laurie had hurt her knee.

8. The doctor said that it would take three months for her knee to _____.

9. Laurie held on to the top of her chair for _____.

10. The bag fell to the floor with a _____.

Exercise D

Using verbs correctly. Fill in the blanks in each sentence to form the **present perfect tense**. Use *has* or *have* plus the **past participle** of the verb in parentheses. Some examples are *has been* and *have* not *gone*. The first sentence has been done for you.

1. Laura ___*has*___ ___*been*___ an ice skater since she was a child. (be)

2. She _____ _____ every competition she entered. (win)

3. She _____ always _____ her best to win. (try)

4. Laurie and Kathy _____ _____ each other since they were children. (know)

5. They _____ _____ together many times. (skate)

6. Laurie and Kathy _____ _____ many skating lessons. (take)

7. Kathy _____ also _____ to a school for skaters. (go)

8. Laurie _____ never _____ a competition. (lose)

9. Through the years, she _____ _____ many fine skaters. (see)

10. Laurie and Jinny _____ never _____ in a competition together. (be)

Write your own sentences in the **present perfect tense** by using the verbs in parentheses.

11. (has brought) _____

_____

12. (have done) _____

_____

13. (has wanted) _____

_____

14. (have bought) _____

_____

15. (has finished) _____

_____

Exercise E

Combining sentences. Combine the two sentences into one by using a comma and the **conjunction** in parentheses (*but, and,* or *so*). Write the sentence on the line. The first one has been done for you.

1. Laurie had been skating very well. Then she hurt her knee. (but)

   Laurie had been skating very well, but then she hurt

   her knee.

2. Laurie didn't know how well she would skate. She was nervous. (so)

3. Laurie had heard about Jinny Jordan. She knew that Jinny was very good. (and)

4. Until the accident Laurie was the one to beat. Now the one to beat was Jinny. (but)

5. Laurie knew the pain would go away. She waited for it to pass. (so)

6. Laurie hoped she wouldn't have to do a triple toe loop. Now she would have to try it. (but)

7. The car in front of them suddenly made a sharp turn. They smashed into it. (and)

Exercise F

Vocabulary review. Write a complete sentence for each word or group of words.

1. opponents _____

_____

2. heal _____

_____

3. predicted _____

_____

4. slippery _____

_____

5. thud _____

_____

6. compete _____

_____

7. examinations _____

_____

8. swerved _____

_____

9. damaged _____

_____

10. doesn't stand a chance _____

_____

SHARING WITH OTHERS

Everyone can learn by sharing ideas. Meet with your partner or group to discuss these questions. Write your answer to one of the questions.

◆ Why did Laurie think it was so important for her to win the competition? Give at least three reasons.

◆ Laurie said, "I saw Jinny skating this morning. She was unbelievable." Briefly describe what Laurie might have seen. First think about all the things that Jinny might have done as she skated. Then write your description.

_____

_____

_____

_____

_____

_____

_____

_____

_____

_____

_____

_____

_____

PART 2

Laurie felt uncomfortable as she looked at Jinny. "So this is my competition," thought Laurie. "Because of her, I may lose tonight."

"I'm Laurie Collins," Laurie told Jinny.

"This **costume** was my mom's idea," Jinny said, looking down at her red, white, and blue skating dress. "I look like a flag. I hope that no one expects me to skate to the music of the 'Star Spangled Banner.'"

Laurie couldn't keep from smiling. She pointed to Jinny's skating bag. "Some stuff fell out of your bag, Jinny," Laurie said. "I guess you didn't have it zipped up all the way."

Jinny looked at the clothing and equipment that lay scattered on the floor. As she began to gather her belongings, the door opened.

"Jinny," called Kathy, "you better give the tape of your music to the sound engineer right away."

"I thought I gave him my music tape half an hour ago," said Jinny. "Tell him it's the green box with my initials written in white in the right-hand corner."

"Maybe you better remind him. He claims you never gave it to him, and he's getting angry."

"Then I don't know what I did with it," said Jinny, hurrying out after Kathy.

Laurie laced her skates. As she did she thought to herself, "That's funny. Jinny has a chance to win tonight, and she doesn't even know what she did with her music."

Laurie knew that music was nearly as important to the program as the skating itself. The music you skated to created mood, rhythm, and style. Laurie had worked with her coach for months to select and then tape her music program. If she lost her music tape, she might as well forget about skating. It was that simple.

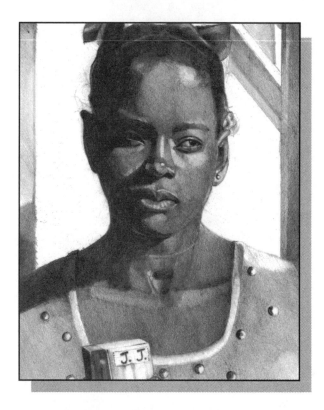

30   Laurie stood up and walked to the chair to do a few more knee
bends. Suddenly she saw something small and dark green behind
the leg of the dressing table. She bent over to pull it out, and saw the
white initials **J. J.** in the top right-hand corner.

"It's Jinny's music tape!" she exclaimed. "It must have rolled out
35   of her bag when she dropped it!"

Laurie stood **motionless** for what must have been only seconds—
yet it seemed like years while she thought about what to do.

"All I'd have to do is forget that I found this," she thought. "If
Jinny doesn't have her music, she might as well not skate. Jinny
40   would look pretty ridiculous skating without music. And then,"
Laurie said to herself, "I would win—because Jinny's the only real
competition I have."

Laurie shivered slightly as she thought about this. Then she
wondered, "Do I really want to win *that* much? Does winning mean
45   so much to me that I'd be willing to cheat for it?"

The door flew open. "Hey, you go on after Jinny," Kathy said.
"Jinny's in real trouble. She still can't find her music."

Laurie hesitated for a second. Then she **pulled herself together**
and said, "Tell Jinny that I found her tape. Would you mind giving it
50   to the sound engineer?"

Minutes later Laurie made her way to the rink. As she moved to
the edge of the ice, she watched Jinny who was skating gracefully to

the sound of the taped music. Laurie looked nervously at Jinny and waited.

55 When the announcer finally called her name, Laurie skated quickly to the center of the rink. She waited until the music filled the stadium. Then, keeping in time with her music, she started with a double toe spin. She immediately followed this by doing a strong spiral on her right leg that carried her round and round across the ice.

60 "Good," she thought to herself, "my knee's holding up."

She felt herself gliding as she spun smoothly out of one figure and into another. The audience applauded from time to time, enthusiastically supporting her in her comeback.

Just before the music ended, she went into a difficult triple toe
65 loop. As she completed it, she heard the audience gasp. When her turn was over, applause filled the stadium, and she stood there, for a moment, in the center of the ice in the spotlight.

As she skated off the ice, she waved to the crowd and quickly made her way to the exit where her coach ran up to her and
70 hugged her.

"You did it, Laurie!" she said. "You skated perfectly—and beautifully. You didn't make a single mistake! I think that you won!"

Laurie said nothing, but she smiled as she **took a seat** and waited to see what marks the judges would give her. When the
75 marks appeared, Laurie knew that she had beaten Jinny Jordan and everyone else.

"Laurie, you won! You won!" Kathy screamed, as she rushed up to her.

"I guess I did," was all Laurie could say.

80 As she walked back to the dressing room, Laurie thought about Jinny's music tape. She remembered wondering whether or not to return it. "But no one will ever know how close I really came to losing," Laurie said softly to herself.

Put an *x* in the box next to the correct answer.

Reading Comprehension

1. Jinny's skating dress was
   - ❑ **a.** black and white.
   - ❑ **b.** green and brown.
   - ❑ **c.** red, white, and blue.

2. Jinny said that her music tape was
   - ❑ **a.** in a green box.
   - ❑ **b.** in her skating bag.
   - ❑ **c.** at her house.

3. Where did Laurie find Jinny's music tape?
   - ❑ **a.** on the chair
   - ❑ **b.** on top of the dressing table
   - ❑ **c.** behind the leg of the dressing table

4. Laurie handed Jinny's tape to
   - ❑ **a.** Kathy.
   - ❑ **b.** Jinny.
   - ❑ **c.** the sound engineer.

5. Before the music ended, Laurie
   - ❑ **a.** fell on the ice.
   - ❑ **b.** did a triple toe loop.
   - ❑ **c.** nearly slipped.

6. Who won the competition?
   - ❑ **a.** Laurie
   - ❑ **b.** Kathy
   - ❑ **c.** Jinny

Vocabulary

7. Jinny's costume made her look like a flag. A *costume* is
   - ❑ **a.** something you wave.
   - ❑ **b.** something you play with.
   - ❑ **c.** something you wear.

8. Laurie stood motionless while she thought about what to do. The word *motionless* means
   - ❑ **a.** without moving.
   - ❑ **b.** sadly.
   - ❑ **c.** with fear.

Idioms

9. Laurie didn't know what to do until she finally pulled herself together. When you *pull yourself together*, you
   - ❑ **a.** lose control of yourself.
   - ❑ **b.** get control of yourself.
   - ❑ **c.** ask for help.

10. Laurie took a seat and waited to see what marks she would get. The idiom *to take a seat* means
    - ❑ **a.** to hide something.
    - ❑ **b.** to steal something.
    - ❑ **c.** to sit down.

How many questions did you answer correctly? Circle your score. Then fill in your score on the Score Chart on page 184.

Number Correct	1	2	3	4	5	6	7	8	9	10
Score	10	20	30	40	50	60	70	80	90	100

EXERCISES TO HELP YOU

Exercise A

Understanding the story. Answer each question by writing a complete sentence. Begin each sentence with a capital letter, and end each sentence with a period. You may use the line numbers in parentheses to help you.

1. What was the color of Jinny's skating dress? (5)

_____

2. What did Jinny think she looked like? (5)

_____

3. What lay scattered on the floor? (11)

_____

_____

4. Who was supposed to get Jinny's music tape? (13)

_____

5. How long had Laurie worked with her coach to select and then tape her music program? (27)

_____

6. What did Laurie see behind the leg of the dressing table? (31)

_____

7. When the announcer called her name, where did Laurie skate? (56)

_____

8. What did Laurie do just before the music ended? (64)

_____

9. To whom did Laurie wave as she skated off the ice? (68)

_____

10. When the marks appeared, what did Laurie know? (75)

_____

_____

Exercise B

Part A

Putting events in order. Put the events in the order in which they occurred. You may look back at the story.

1. ____
2. ____
3. ____
4. ____
5. ____
6. ____
7. ____
8. ____

a. Laurie gave Jinny's music tape to Kathy.

b. Laurie's coach hugged her.

c. Kathy said the engineer needed Jinny's music tape.

d. Laurie found Jinny's music tape.

e. Jinny gathered some things that had fallen out of her skating bag.

f. When the announcer called her name, Laurie began to skate.

g. Kathy said that Laurie had won.

h. Laurie did a triple toe loop.

Part B

Now list the correct order of the events on the lines below.

1. _____

   _____

2. _____

3. _____

4. _____

5. _____

   _____

6. _____

7. _____

8. _____

Exercise C

Adding vocabulary. On the left are 10 words from the story. Complete each sentence by adding the correct word.

stadium

applauded

initials

spiral

zipped

ridiculous

select

mood

hesitated

belongings

1. Something fell out of Jinny's bag because she didn't

   have it _____ up all the way.

2. Laurie thought that Jinny would look

   _____ skating without music.

3. She knew that the music you skated to created a certain

   _____.

4. Laurie worked with her coach for months to

   _____ just the right music.

5. Jinny picked up her clothing and other

   _____ that had fallen to the floor.

6. Laurie found a box with the _____ **J. J.** in

   the corner.

7. Laurie didn't answer immediately; she

   _____ before speaking.

8. Laurie waited until the music filled the large

   _____.

9. Laurie did a _____ that carried her round

   and round across the ice.

10. From time to time the audience _____

    Laurie's skating.

Exercise D

Using verbs correctly. Fill in each blank with the **past tense** of the irregular verb or verbs in parentheses.

1. Laurie _____ uncomfortable as she looked at Jinny. (feel)

2. Jinny _____ a dress that _____ very bright colors. (wear, have)

3. Something _____ out of Jinny's skating bag. (fall)

4. Jinny _____ that she _____ her music tape to the sound engineer. (think, give)

5. Laurie _____ up and walked to the chair. (stand)

6. The door suddenly _____ open and Kathy _____ into the room. (fly, come)

7. Laurie _____ the dressing room and _____ to the rink. (leave, go)

8. After the music _____, Laurie started to skate. (begin)

9. Laurie's coach _____ up to Laurie and hugged her. (run)

10. When the marks appeared, Laurie _____ that she _____ the competition. (know, win)

Write your own sentences in the **past tense** by using the verbs in parentheses.

11. (forgot) _____

_____

12. (could) _____

_____

13. (brought) _____

_____

14. (wrote) _____

_____

15. (chose) _____

_____

Exercise E

Adding apostrophes. Correct the following sentences by adding **apostrophes** to show possession. Write the corrected sentences on the lines. The first one has been done for you.

1. Suddenly Laurie noticed Jinnys music tape.

   Suddenly Laurie noticed Jinny's music tape.

2. Laurie could see Kathys face in the crowd.

   _____.

3. When Laurie heard the announcers voice, she stepped onto the ice.

   _____

   _____.

4. Lauries coach thought that Laurie had skated perfectly.

   _____.

5. Jinny said, "This costume was my moms idea."

   _____.

Correct the following sentences by adding **apostrophes** to show **contractions.** Be sure to put the apostrophe in the correct place. Write the corrected sentences on the lines. The first one has been done for you.

6. Jinny didnt know what she did with her music tape.

   Jinny didn't know what she did with her music tape.

7. She is worried because she cant skate without music.

   _____.

8. "I dont know where it is," Jinny told Kathy.

   _____.

9. Laurie knows that its important to have the right music.

   _____.

10. Kathy doesnt skate as well as Laurie or Jinny.

   _____.

Exercise F

Vocabulary review. Write a complete sentence for each word or group of words.

1. applauded _____

   _____

2. ridiculous _____

   _____

3. stadium _____

   _____

4. hesitated _____

   _____

5. belongings _____

   _____

6. initials _____

   _____

7. mood _____

   _____

8. costume _____

   _____

9. took a seat _____

   _____

10. pulled herself together _____

   _____

SHARING WITH OTHERS

Everyone can learn by sharing ideas. Meet with your partner or group to discuss these questions. Write your answer to one of the questions.

◆ If you were Laurie, would you have returned Jinny's music tape? Why?

◆ Laurie won the skating competition. But as she walked to the dressing room, she thought about the music tape and said, "No one will ever know how close I really came to losing." What did Laurie mean by this?

_____

_____

_____

_____

_____

_____

_____

_____

_____

_____

_____

_____

_____

GOD SEES THE TRUTH, BUT WAITS

by Leo Tolstoy

GOD SEES THE TRUTH, BUT WAITS

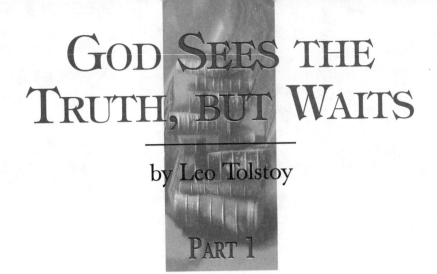

by Leo Tolstoy

PART 1

Leo Tolstoy, the great Russian writer, was interested in the meaning of life. This story is a good example of his writing.

In the town of Vladimir in Russia there lived a wealthy young merchant named Ivan Aksenoff. He owned two shops and a large house.

Aksenoff was a handsome, blond, curly-haired fellow who loved
5   to have fun and was very fond of singing. Years ago, when he was much younger, he sometimes drank too much and got into trouble. But after he got married, he gave up drinking.

One summer afternoon, Aksenoff was preparing to go to the fair[1] at Nizhny where he hoped to sell his **merchandise**. As he was
10   saying good-bye to his family, his wife said to him, "Ivan, please do not go to the fair today. I dreamed that something bad happened to you there. For my sake, please stay at home."

Aksenoff laughed and said, "You know that I **have got to** go to the fair. What are you afraid of?"

15   His wife replied, "I do not know what I am afraid of. All I know is that I had a bad dream. I dreamed that you were coming home from the fair, and when you took off your cap, I saw that your hair had turned gray."

Aksenoff laughed and said, "That means good luck. You'll see.
20   I'll sell everything I bring to the fair, and I'll come home with some wonderful presents for you all."

Then Ivan kissed his wife and children, said good-bye, and departed.

When he had traveled halfway to Nizhny, he met a merchant he

---

1. *fair:* As used here, the word means "a place where people gather to buy and sell things."

25 knew and they stopped at an inn[2] for the night. They discussed business for a while. Then they had some tea together, and each man went to bed in separate rooms.

Aksenoff woke up before dawn. Knowing that it would be pleasant to travel while it was still cool, he went to the office and
30 paid his bill. Then he got his horses and continued on his journey.

When he had gone about twenty-five miles, he stopped at another inn and asked to have his horses fed. Aksenoff went out onto the porch, ordered some tea, and took out his guitar and began to play.

35 Suddenly, a carriage with three horses came **dashing** up to the inn. A police officer and two soldiers rushed out of the carriage. The officer walked straight up to Aksenoff and began to question him. The officer asked him who he was and where he had come from. Aksenoff answered the officer's questions fully. Then Aksenoff said,
40 "Would you like to have some tea with me?" But the officer ignored this and began to ask him more questions. He asked, "Where did you spend last night? Did you speak to another merchant? Did you see the other merchant this morning? Why did you leave the inn before dawn?"

45 Aksenoff wondered why the officer was asking him all these questions, but he described in detail everything that had happened. Then he asked, "Why are you **cross-examining** me as if I were a thief? I am a merchant traveling on business. There is no reason for you to question me."

2. *inn:* a place where travelers can get meals and a room to sleep in.

Then the officer said, "I am the Chief of Police in this district, and I am questioning you because the merchant with whom you had tea last night has been murdered. We must search your things."

The soldiers and the Chief unstrapped Aksenoff's luggage and began searching through his belongings. Suddenly, the Chief pulled a knife out of Aksenoff's things. "Whose knife is this?" the Chief demanded.

Aksenoff stared, shocked and amazed, at the bloodstained knife that had been taken out of his bag.

"And whose blood is on the knife?" the Chief of Police asked, sharply.

Aksenoff tried to answer, but he was so frightened he could hardly utter a word. He began to stammer, "I—I—do not know. That—that knife does—does not—belong to me."

The Chief continued, "The merchant was found dead this morning. He had been stabbed to death in his bed. Now we find this bloodstained knife among your possessions. You are nervous and have a guilty look on your face. Tell me at once how you murdered the merchant and how much money you stole from him!"

Aksenoff swore that he had not committed the murder and that the knife was not his. He swore that he had not seen the merchant after they drank tea together, and that the only money he had was 8,000 rubles of his own. But Aksenoff's voice kept breaking, his face was very pale, and he shook with fear as though he were guilty.

The Chief ordered the soldiers to tie up Aksenoff and to put him in the carriage. All of his money and his goods were taken away from him, and he was sent to a nearby town and was thrown into jail. A trial was held and he was convicted of murdering the merchant and stealing his money.

Put an *x* in the box next to the correct answer.

Reading Comprehension

1. Aksenoff's wife didn't want him to go to the fair because she
   - ❑ **a.** needed his help at home.
   - ❑ **b.** didn't think he would sell anything there.
   - ❑ **c.** dreamed that something bad happened to him there.

2. Aksenoff said that he would come home with
   - ❑ **a.** a friend.
   - ❑ **b.** wonderful presents.
   - ❑ **c.** gray hair.

3. Aksenoff met a merchant he knew and they
   - ❑ **a.** had tea together.
   - ❑ **b.** ate dinner together.
   - ❑ **c.** went to a show together.

4. The Chief of Police stated that a merchant
   - ❑ **a.** had been murdered.
   - ❑ **b.** was missing.
   - ❑ **c.** said that Aksenoff stole his money.

5. What did they find among Aksenoff's things?
   - ❑ **a.** a gun
   - ❑ **b.** a bloody knife
   - ❑ **c.** 10,000 rubles

6. What happened to Aksenoff at the end of Part 1?
   - ❑ **a.** The Chief let him go home.
   - ❑ **b.** He ran away.
   - ❑ **c.** He was thrown in jail.

Vocabulary

7. Aksenoff hoped that he would sell his merchandise at the fair. The word *merchandise* means
   - ❑ **a.** horses or cows.
   - ❑ **b.** things that are for sale.
   - ❑ **c.** a small amount of money.

8. Three horses came dashing up to the house. The word *dashing* means
   - ❑ **a.** rushing or hurrying.
   - ❑ **b.** yelling or shouting.
   - ❑ **c.** falling down.

9. "Why are you cross-examining me as if I were a thief?" The word *cross-examining* means
   - ❑ **a.** hitting.
   - ❑ **b.** pushing.
   - ❑ **c.** questioning.

Idioms

10. Aksenoff said, "I have got to go to the fair." The idiom *have got to* means
    - ❑ **a.** must.
    - ❑ **b.** won't.
    - ❑ **c.** forgot.

How many questions did you answer correctly? Circle your score. Then fill in your score on the Score Chart on page 184.

Number Correct	1	2	3	4	5	6	7	8	9	10
Score	10	20	30	40	50	60	70	80	90	100

Exercise A

Understanding the story. Answer each question by writing a complete sentence. Begin each sentence with a capital letter, and end each sentence with a period. You may use the line numbers in parentheses to help you.

1. Where did Aksenoff live? (1)

_____

2. What did Aksenoff own? (2)

_____

3. In his wife's dream, what happened to Aksenoff's hair? (17)

_____

4. What did Aksenoff say he would bring home? (20)

_____

5. Whom did Aksenoff meet when he had traveled halfway to Nizhny? (24)

_____

6. What did Aksenoff and the merchant discuss? (25)

_____

7. Who rushed out of the carriage? (36)

_____

_____

8. What did the Chief pull out of Aksenoff's things? (55)

_____

9. What did the Chief order the soldiers to do? (74)

_____

10. Where was Aksenoff sent? (76)

_____

Exercise B

Part A

Putting events in order. Put the events in the order in which they occurred. You may look back at the story.

1. ____

2. ____

3. ____

4. ____

5. ____

6. ____

7. ____

a. Aksenoff had tea with a merchant.

b. The Chief found a knife among Aksenoff's things.

c. Aksenoff paid his bill and went on his way.

d. Aksenoff's wife asked him not to go to the fair.

e. A police officer and two soldiers rushed out of a carriage.

f. Aksenoff was thrown into jail.

g. Aksenoff kissed his wife and children and left for the fair.

Part B

Now list the correct order of the events on the lines below.

1. _____

2. _____

   _____

3. _____

4. _____

5. _____

   _____

6. _____

7. _____

Exercise C

Adding vocabulary. On the left are 10 words from the story. Complete each sentence by adding the correct word.

luggage

district

dawn

detail

journey

committed

guitar

convicted

guilty

ignored

1. Aksenoff wanted to travel while it was still early, so he

   left before _____.

2. He paid his bill, got his horses, and continued on his

   _____.

3. Aksenoff ordered some tea, took out his

   _____, and began to play.

4. An officer said, "I am the Police Chief in this

   _____."

5. Aksenoff carefully described in _____

   everything that had happened.

6. Aksenoff was nervous, and he had a _____

   look on his face.

7. The officer did not listen to Aksenoff; the officer

   _____ him.

8. They looked through Aksenoff's trunks and bags;

   they looked through his _____.

9. Aksenoff swore that he had not _____

   the murder.

10. He was _____ of killing the merchant and

    stealing his money.

Exercise D

Using verbs correctly. Fill in each blank using the **past tense** of the regular (1–10) and irregular (11–20) verb or verbs in parentheses.

1. Aksenoff _____ singing and _____ to have fun. (enjoy, love)

2. Aksenoff's wife _____ that his hair _____ gray. (dream, turn)

3. He _____ at an inn and _____ some tea. (stop, order)

4. Aksenoff _____ business with a merchant. (discuss)

5. Two soldiers _____ out of the carriage. (rush)

6. Aksenoff _____ why they were asking him so many questions. (wonder)

7. Aksenoff _____ the officer's questions. (answer)

8. They _____ through his things and _____ a knife. (search, discover)

9. "Whose knife is this?" the Chief _____. (demand)

10. He said that Aksenoff _____ the merchant. (murder)

11. When he was young, Aksenoff _____ too much. (drink)

12. After he _____ married, Aksenoff _____ up drinking. (get, give)

13. His wife _____ that she _____ a bad dream. (say, have)

14. On his way to Nizhny, Aksenoff _____ a merchant. (meet)

15. He _____ up early, _____ to the office, and _____ his bill. (wake, go, pay)

16. At the inn, they _____ his horses. (feed)

17. The officers _____ to question Aksenoff. (begin)

18. He _____ that he had not murdered the merchant. (swear)

19. They _____ away his money and _____ him into jail. (take, throw)

20. They _____ him to a nearby town where they _____ a trial. (send, hold)

Exercise E
Picking a possessive. Fill in each blank by adding the correct
possessive. Use each possessive once.

my	**his**	**your**	**their**
mine	**her**	**its**	**theirs**

1. Ivan Aksenoff owned a house and two shops. They were _____.

2. Aksenoff's wife told him about _____ dream.

3. She said, "When you took off your hat, I saw that _____ hair had turned gray."

4. When the merchants went to the fair, they took _____ horses and merchandise with them.

5. The Chief found a knife in Aksenoff's bag. The Chief held the knife

   carefully by _____ handle.

6. Aksenoff was shocked when he saw the knife. He said, "That knife is

   not _____."

7. Aksenoff swore he did not have the merchant's money. "This is

   _____ money," he told the Chief.

8. All of the merchandise belonged to the merchants. It was

   _____.

Exercise F

Vocabulary review. Write a complete sentence for each word or group of words.

1. guilty _____

_____

2. luggage _____

_____

3. committed _____

_____

4. guitar _____

_____

5. ignored _____

_____

6. district _____

_____

7. convicted _____

_____

8. merchandise _____

_____

9. cross-examining _____

_____

10. have got to _____

_____

SHARING WITH OTHERS

Everyone can learn by sharing ideas. Meet with your partner or group to discuss these questions. Write your answer to one of the questions.

◆ Aksenoff's wife told Aksenoff that she dreamed his hair had turned gray. Why did she think that meant something bad would happen to him? Why did he think that it meant good luck?

◆ Aksenoff was convicted of murdering the merchant and stealing his money. Why do you think Aksenoff was convicted? List all of the things that suggested that Aksenoff killed the merchant.

_____

_____

_____

_____

_____

_____

_____

_____

_____

_____

_____

_____

_____

PART 2

When Aksenoff's wife heard that her husband was in jail, she did not know what to believe. Her children were all very young—one was still a baby. She took them all with her and went to the town where her husband was in prison.

At first she was not allowed to see Aksenoff, but finally she was given permission to see him. When she saw him in prison clothes with chains on his feet, she fainted and fell to the floor. After she got up, she gathered her children to her and sat down with them by her husband's side. She told him how things were back home and asked him what had happened. He told her everything that had taken place. Then she asked, "What can we do now?"

"We must send a letter to the King," he said. "We must ask him to set me free. Surely they will not let an innocent man be punished."

His wife said that she had already sent a petition to the King, and that the King refused to consider[1] his case.

Aksenoff did not reply and stared sadly at the floor.

Then his wife said, "You remember I dreamed that your hair had turned gray. You remember my dream? Ah, if only you had stayed home that day." Then she said softly, "Ivan, my dear husband, tell me the truth. Did you murder the merchant?"

"So you do not believe me either!" cried Aksenoff, and covering his face with his hands, he **burst into tears**. Then a guard came to the cell and said that it was time for his wife and children to leave. So, for the last time, Aksenoff said good-bye to his family.

1. *consider:* think about.

When they were gone, Aksenoff thought about his wife's visit. He remembered that even she suspected him of killing the merchant. Then he said to himself, "It appears that only God knows the truth. God is the one to ask for mercy and the only one who can give it."

30　　Aksenoff was sent to a prison camp in Siberia. For twenty-six years he lived there as a convict.[2] The hair on his head turned as white as snow, and his beard grew very long. He walked slowly, seldom spoke, never laughed, and prayed often.

Over the years, no news reached Aksenoff from his home. He 35　did not even know if his wife and children were still alive.

Then one day a group of new convicts was brought into the prison. In the evening, the old prisoners gathered around the new ones and asked them where they came from and why they had been sent to the prison camp. Aksenoff sat down near the **newcomers** 40　and, with his eyes staring at the floor, listened to what they said.

One of the new convicts was a tall, strong, and **vigorous** man who was about sixty years old.

2. *convict:* a person who is in jail for a crime.

"Well, friends," he was saying, "the truth is I was sent here for nothing. I borrowed a horse that belonged to a friend, but I was arrested and was accused[3] of stealing it. I explained that I took it because I was **in a hurry** to get home and that I was going to return it later. I kept telling them that the horse belonged to a friend of mine. But they insisted[4] I had stolen it."

The man shook his head and smiled.

"It's funny," he said, "because once I really *did* do something that was wrong. But that time they didn't catch me. And now I have been sent here for doing nothing at all. Ah, well, life is hard to explain."

"Where are you from?" someone asked.

"I come from Vladimir. My name is Makar Semevitch."

When he heard that, Aksenoff raised his head and said, "Tell me, Semevitch, do you know anything about a family named Aksenoff? Have you heard of them? They were merchants in Vladimir. Are they still alive?"

"Have I heard of them? Of course I have! The old woman is dead. But the children have worked hard and are rich, though their father is in Siberia. He is a convict like us, it seems. But you—for what crime did they send you here?"

Aksenoff did not say anything for a long time. He did not like to speak about his misfortune. He only sighed and said, "I have been in prison for twenty-six years."

"But what did you do? What was your crime?" Makar Semevitch asked.

Aksenoff was silent and would say no more. But the other convicts told Semevitch why Aksenoff was sent to Siberia—how someone had killed a merchant and had put the knife among Aksenoff's things.

When Semevitch heard this he looked closely at Aksenoff, slapped himself on his knee, and exclaimed, "Well, this is amazing! Really remarkable!" Then he said softly to himself, "But how old you've become."

The other prisoners asked Semevitch why he seemed so surprised, but Semevitch did not answer.

3. *accused:* blamed.
4. *insisted:* kept saying.

Aksenoff wondered whether this man knew who had killed the merchant, so he said, "Semevitch, perhaps you have heard of that crime."

80

"Heard of it! Of course I have heard of it! It was on everyone's lips at the time. But that was long ago, and I don't remember much about it now."

"Perhaps you know who really killed the merchant," Aksenoff said slowly.

85

Semevitch laughed and said, "Well, it is obvious that the man who killed him was the man who was found with the bloody knife. Look, how could anyone put a knife into your bag while you were asleep? That would surely have woken you up."

90

When Aksenoff heard these words, he felt certain that *this* was the man who had killed the merchant! He got up and walked slowly away. And all that night Aksenoff could not sleep.

Put an *x* in the box next to the correct answer.

Reading Comprehension

1. Aksenoff's wife went to the jail with
   - ❑ **a.** some friends.
   - ❑ **b.** her parents.
   - ❑ **c.** her children.

2. Aksenoff's wife asked him if he
   - ❑ **a.** was getting enough food.
   - ❑ **b.** had killed the merchant.
   - ❑ **c.** would be home soon.

3. Aksenoff lived in Siberia
   - ❑ **a.** about ten years.
   - ❑ **b.** twenty-six years.
   - ❑ **c.** thirty years.

4. The police said that Semevitch
   - ❑ **a.** stole a horse.
   - ❑ **b.** killed a man.
   - ❑ **c.** stole some money.

5. Aksenoff learned that
   - ❑ **a.** his wife was still alive.
   - ❑ **b.** his children had died.
   - ❑ **c.** his children were rich.

6. Which statement is true?
   - ❑ **a.** Aksenoff liked Semevitch.
   - ❑ **b.** Aksenoff believed what Semevitch said.
   - ❑ **c.** Aksenoff thought Semevitch had killed the merchant.

Vocabulary

7. New convicts were brought in. Aksenoff sat down near the newcomers. What are *newcomers*?
   - ❑ **a.** people who have just arrived
   - ❑ **b.** people who are young
   - ❑ **c.** people who have done something wrong

8. One of the convicts was a man who was strong and vigorous. The word *vigorous* means
   - ❑ **a.** very sad.
   - ❑ **b.** powerful and full of life.
   - ❑ **c.** quiet and shy.

Idioms

9. Aksenoff covered his face with his hands and burst into tears. The idiom *burst into tears* means
   - ❑ **a.** fell asleep.
   - ❑ **b.** dropped to the ground.
   - ❑ **c.** suddenly began to cry.

10. Semevitch took a horse because he was in a hurry to get home. When you are *in a hurry*, you
    - ❑ **a.** move quickly.
    - ❑ **b.** are in trouble.
    - ❑ **c.** are in a crowd.

How many questions did you answer correctly? Circle your score. Then fill in your score on the Score Chart on page 184.

Number Correct	1	2	3	4	5	6	7	8	9	10
Score	10	20	30	40	50	60	70	80	90	100

Exercise A

Understanding the story. Answer each question by writing a complete sentence. Begin each sentence with a capital letter, and end each sentence with a period. You may use the line numbers in parentheses to help you.

1. When Aksenoff's wife went to the jail, who did she take with her? (3)

   _____

2. What did Aksenoff want to send to the King? (12)

   _____

3. Where was Aksenoff sent? (30)

   _____

4. How long did he live there? (30)

   _____

5. What happened to the hair on Aksenoff's head? (31)

   _____

6. How often did Aksenoff laugh? (33)

   _____

7. How old was Makar Semevitch? (42)

   _____

8. What town did Semevitch come from? (54)

   _____

9. What happened to Aksenoff's children? (60)

   _____

10. Who did Aksenoff think killed the merchant? (90)

    _____

    _____

Exercise B

Part A

Putting events in order. Put the events in the order in which they occurred. You may look back at the story.

1. ____

2. ____

3. ____

4. ____

5. ____

6. ____

7. ____

8. ____

a. The guard told Aksenoff's wife to leave.

b. Aksenoff left Semevitch and could not sleep.

c. Aksenoff's wife asked him if he had murdered the merchant.

d. Aksenoff asked Semevitch if he had heard about a family named Aksenoff.

e. Aksenoff's wife went to the prison in the town.

f. Semevitch said the murderer was the man who was found with the bloody knife.

g. New convicts arrived at the prison.

h. Aksenoff was sent to a prison camp in Siberia.

Part B

Now list the correct order of the events on the lines below.

1. _____

2. _____

_____

3. _____

4. _____

5. _____

6. _____

_____

7. _____

_____

8. _____

Exercise C

Adding vocabulary. On the left are 10 words from the story. Complete each sentence by adding the correct word.

innocent

fainted

permission

refused

petition

obvious

reply

remarkable

suspected

misfortune

1. At first Aksenoff's wife could not see him, but later she was given _____ to visit.

2. When Aksenoff's wife saw him in prison clothes, she _____ and fell to the ground.

3. Aksenoff hoped that he would be set free because he knew that he was an _____ man.

4. Aksenoff wanted to send a letter to the King, but his wife had already sent the King a _____.

5. The King said no to the letter. He _____ to consider it.

6. Aksenoff did not answer his wife; he did not _____.

7. Everyone thought that Aksenoff had killed the merchant. Even Aksenoff's wife _____ him.

8. Semevitch said, "It is _____ that the man who killed the merchant was the man who had the bloody knife."

9. Aksenoff did not like to talk about his bad luck, so he never discussed his _____.

10. Semevitch slapped himself on the knee and said, "Why this is amazing—really _____!"

Exercise D

Using verbs correctly. Fill in the blanks in each sentence to form the **past perfect tense**. Remember to use *had* plus the **past participle** of the verb in parentheses.

1. Aksenoff told his wife everything that _____ _____ place. (take)

2. His wife _____ already _____ a petition to the King. (send)

3. She told Aksenoff, "If only you _____ _____ home that day." (stay)

4. The murderer _____ _____ the knife among Aksenoff's things. (put)

5. Semevitch said that he _____ not _____ the horse. (steal)

6. Aksenoff asked Semevitch if he _____ _____ of the Aksenoff family. (hear)

7. Semevitch stated that the old woman _____ _____. (die)

8. Aksenoff wondered if Semevitch knew who _____ _____ the merchant. (kill)

Fill in the blanks in each sentence to form the **present perfect tense**. Remember to use *has* or *have* plus the **past participle** of the verb in parentheses.

9. Aksenoff said, "For twenty-six years I _____ _____ in prison." (be)

10. Since he arrived in prison, Aksenoff _____ not _____ his children. (see)

11. He _____ never _____ home to visit his family. (go)

12. His children _____ often _____ about their father. (think)

13. Semevitch said, "The children _____ _____ hard and are rich." (work)

14. Aksenoff _____ always _____ to be a good prisoner. (try)

15. Semevitch said, "If someone had put a knife in your bag, that would surely _____ _____ you up." (wake)

Exercise E

Part A

True or false statements. Write **T** if the sentence is true. Write **F** if the sentence is false.

1. _____ Aksenoff's wife fainted when she saw him in jail.

2. _____ The King said that he would consider Aksenoff's case.

3. _____ Aksenoff's hair turned white, and his beard grew long.

4. _____ Aksenoff walked slowly and seldom spoke.

5. _____ Both Aksenoff and Semevitch came from Vladimir.

6. _____ Semevitch arrived at the prison with some new convicts.

7. _____ Aksenoff discovered that his children were poor.

8. _____ Semevitch thought that Aksenoff looked very young.

9. _____ Semevitch said that he had heard about the crime.

10. _____ Aksenoff had been in prison for thirty-six years.

Part B

On the lines below, correct the false statements.

a. _____

_____

b. _____

_____

c. _____

_____

d. _____

_____

Exercise F

Vocabulary review. Write a complete sentence for each word or group of words.

1. suspected _____

_____

2. permission _____

_____

3. innocent _____

_____

4. fainted _____

_____

5. refused _____

_____

6. misfortune _____

_____

7. newcomers _____

_____

8. vigorous _____

_____

9. in a hurry _____

_____

10. burst into tears _____

_____

SHARING WITH OTHERS

Everyone can learn by sharing ideas. Meet with your partner or group to discuss these questions. Write your answer to one of the questions.

◆ Do you think that Aksenoff's wife believed that her husband was innocent—or did she believe that he killed the merchant? Give reasons for your answer.

◆ Aksenoff felt certain that Semevitch was the man who had killed the merchant. What clues in the story suggest that Semevitch was the murderer?

_____

_____

_____

_____

_____

_____

_____

_____

_____

_____

_____

_____

_____

_____

PART 3

Aksenoff could not sleep that night. He was extremely unhappy and he thought about many things. He saw the **image** of his wife as she was when he left her to go to the fair at Nizhny. He remembered her face and her eyes and her voice. Then he remembered his children, who were very small at that time. And then he remembered himself as he used to be—young and happy. He remembered how he had sat on the porch of the inn where they had arrested him, how he had played his guitar, and how cheerful he had been.

Then he thought about the trial and about the terrible crime they said he had committed. He remembered the people staring at him and the chains he had worn. He thought about the twenty-six years he had been in prison, and about how old he had become. The thought of it filled him with **grief**.

"And it's all *his* fault!" thought Aksenoff. And he was furious at Makar Semevitch and wanted revenge. He could not go near the man. He could not even look at him.

One evening as Aksenoff was wandering sadly around the prison, he noticed some earth on the floor near one of the bunks. As he was staring at it, Makar Semevitch suddenly crawled out from under the bunk and glared up at Aksenoff with a startled look on his face.

Before Aksenoff could take another step, Semevitch grabbed him by the arm and told him that he had been digging a tunnel under the wall. Semevitch said that he had been disposing of the earth by putting it into his boots and then emptying it out later on the road when the prisoners were marching to work.

"Keep quiet, old man, and I'll get you out of here too!" he

whispered, threateningly. "If you tell them what I've been doing, they'll beat the life out of me. But **bear in mind**, I'll kill you first!" he warned.

Aksenoff, filled with rage, looked at his enemy and angrily said, "I have nothing to gain by escaping. And as for killing me—you killed me long ago!" Then, pulling his arm fiercely away from Semevitch, Aksenoff walked quickly away.

The next day while the convicts were being taken to work, a guard noticed some fresh earth scattered on the road. The prison was searched, and the tunnel was discovered. The warden arrived and began to question each prisoner to find out who had dug the passage. No one admitted that he had dug the tunnel or accused anyone else of digging it.

Finally the warden came to Aksenoff.

"I know that you are a truthful old man," said the warden. "Tell me who dug the tunnel."

Makar Semevitch was standing nearby. He tried to appear unconcerned, but his heart was pounding with fear. He did not dare to look at the warden or at Aksenoff.

Aksenoff's lips and hands trembled. A long time passed before he could speak. He was thinking, "Why should I protect the man who has ruined my life? I should make him pay, at last, for all my suffering! But if I tell, they'll probably beat him to death. And what difference would that make? What good would that be to me?"

"Well, old man," repeated the warden, "tell us the truth. Who dug the tunnel?"

Aksenoff glanced at Makar Semevitch and replied, "I cannot say. I cannot say, your honor. Do whatever you want with me."

And despite all of the warden's threats, Aksenoff said nothing more. As a result, they failed to discover who had dug the tunnel.

That night, as Aksenoff was lying on his bunk, someone approached him and sat at his feet. Aksenoff **peered** through the darkness and recognized Semevitch.

"What more do you want of me?" asked Aksenoff. "Why have you come here?"

Makar Semevitch was silent, so Aksenoff sat up and said, "What do you want? Go away or I will call the guard!"

Makar Semevitch leaned close to Aksenoff and whispered, "Ivan Aksenoff, forgive me!"

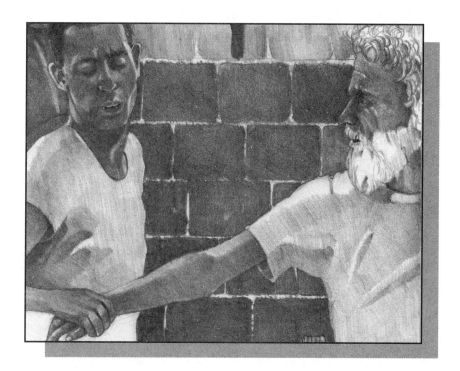

"Forgive you for what?"

"It was I who killed the merchant and hid the knife among your things. I was going to kill you too, but I heard a noise outside. So I hid the knife in your bag and escaped through the window."

Aksenoff was silent and did not know what to say. Makar Semevitch knelt upon the ground. "Ivan Aksenoff," he said, "forgive me. Please forgive me. I will confess that I killed the merchant, and you will be released and can go back to your home."

"It is easy for you to say that," said Aksenoff, "but I have suffered for you these twenty-six years. Where could I go now? My wife is dead, and my children have forgotten me. I have nowhere to go."

Makar Semevitch bowed his head.

"Ivan Aksenoff, forgive me!" he cried. "The worst beating they could give me would be easier to take than to look at you now. You had pity on me and did not tell them that I dug the tunnel. Forgive me! Please forgive me!" And he began to sob.

When Aksenoff heard him sobbing, he too began to weep.

"God will forgive you," said Aksenoff.

At these words Aksenoff's heart grew light, and he suddenly felt a wonderful peace and freedom in his soul.

The next day, Makar Semevitch confessed to the crime. But when the order came to release the innocent man, Ivan Aksenoff was already dead.

YOU CAN ANSWER THESE QUESTIONS

Put an *x* in the box next to the correct answer.

Reading Comprehension

1. Aksenoff could not sleep at night because he was
- ❑ **a.** hungry.
- ❑ **b.** cold.
- ❑ **c.** very unhappy.

2. Aksenoff noticed some earth
- ❑ **a.** in the yard of the prison.
- ❑ **b.** on the floor of the prison.
- ❑ **c.** on the road to the prison.

3. Semevitch told Aksenoff that he had been
- ❑ **a.** digging a tunnel.
- ❑ **b.** planning to climb over the wall.
- ❑ **c.** planning to break down the wall.

4. Semevitch was afraid that Aksenoff would
- ❑ **a.** beat him to death.
- ❑ **b.** tell what he had done.
- ❑ **c.** yell at him.

5. After he killed the merchant, why didn't Semevitch kill Aksenoff?
- ❑ **a.** Noise from outside scared him away.
- ❑ **b.** He suddenly felt sorry for Aksenoff.
- ❑ **c.** He thought that Aksenoff might help him later.

6. At the end of the story, Ivan Aksenoff
- ❑ **a.** returned to his home.
- ❑ **b.** wrote to his children.
- ❑ **c.** died.

Vocabulary

7. When Aksenoff thought about his wife, he saw her image. The word *image* means
- ❑ **a.** picture.
- ❑ **b.** children.
- ❑ **c.** house.

8. He thought about how old he had become and was filled with grief. The word *grief* means
- ❑ **a.** joy.
- ❑ **b.** time.
- ❑ **c.** sadness.

9. Aksenoff peered through the darkness and saw Semevitch. The word *peered* means
- ❑ **a.** worried about.
- ❑ **b.** looked closely.
- ❑ **c.** was frightened.

Idioms

10. "If you tell them what I did, they'll beat me. But bear in mind, I'll kill you first." The idiom *bear in mind* means
- ❑ **a.** don't forget.
- ❑ **b.** ask about.
- ❑ **c.** look around.

How many questions did you answer correctly? Circle your score. Then fill in your score on the Score Chart on page 184.

Number Correct	1	2	3	4	5	6	7	8	9	10
Score	10	20	30	40	50	60	70	80	90	100

EXERCISES TO HELP YOU

Exercise A

Understanding the story. Answer each question by writing a complete sentence. Begin each sentence with a capital letter, and end each sentence with a period. You may use the line numbers in parentheses to help you.

1. What did Aksenoff notice as he was wandering around the prison? (18)

_____

2. What had Semevitch been digging? (23)

_____

3. What did a guard notice on the road? (36)

_____

4. What happened when the prison was searched? (37)

_____

5. What did the warden want to know? (38)

_____

6. What did Semevitch do with the knife? (70)

_____

7. How long had Aksenoff suffered? (76)

_____

8. Why couldn't Aksenoff go back to his family? (76)

_____

_____

9. What did Aksenoff do when he heard Semevitch weeping? (83)

_____

10. What happened to Aksenoff at the end of the story? (88)

_____

Exercise B

Part A

Putting events in order. Put the events in the order in which they occurred. You may look back at the story.

1. ____
2. ____
3. ____
4. ____
5. ____
6. ____
7. ____
8. ____

a. The prison was searched, and the tunnel was discovered.

b. The warden asked Aksenoff to tell him who dug the tunnel.

c. Aksenoff was very unhappy and could not sleep.

d. Semevitch told Aksenoff that he had killed the merchant.

e. Aksenoff noticed some earth near one of the bunks.

f. Aksenoff would not tell the warden who dug the tunnel.

g. The order came, but Aksenoff was dead.

h. Semevitch said that he had been digging a tunnel.

Part B

Now list the correct order of the events on the lines below.

1. _____
2. _____
3. _____
4. _____
   _____
5. _____
   _____
6. _____
   _____
7. _____
8. _____

Exercise C

Adding vocabulary. On the left are 10 words from the story. Complete each sentence by adding the correct word.

trembled

admitted

startled

revenge

bunk

threateningly

confess

glared

release

disposing

1. Semevitch caused Aksenoff so much pain that Aksenoff wanted _____.

2. Semevitch suddenly crawled out from under a _____.

3. Semevitch looked angrily at Aksenoff; Semevitch _____ at him.

4. Since Semevitch was surprised, he had a _____ look on his face.

5. He had been _____ of the earth by emptying it on the road.

6. "If you tell them what I've been doing, I'll kill you," he said, _____.

7. No one _____ that he had dug the tunnel.

8. Aksenoff was shaking; his lips and hands _____.

9. Semevitch told Aksenoff, "I will _____ that I killed the merchant."

10. When the order came to _____ Aksenoff, he was already dead.

Exercise D

Using verbs correctly. Fill in each blank by writing **present, past,** or **future** to show the tense of the verb in each sentence. The first one has been done for you.

1. Tomorrow Semevitch will speak to the warden. _____*future*_____

2. Semevitch will tell the warden about Aksenoff. _____

3. Aksenoff thought about his children. _____

4. He remembers his wife's face. _____

5. Semevitch sat at Aksenoff's feet. _____

6. The warden asks the prisoners about the tunnel. _____

7. Aksenoff will visit his children in Vladimir. _____

8. The prisoners stare silently at Aksenoff. _____

9. Semevitch heard a noise outside the window. _____

10. Now Aksenoff is a free man. _____

Fill in each blank by writing **present perfect**, **past perfect**, or **past continuous** to show the tense of the verb in each sentence. The first one has been done for you.

11. Aksenoff was wandering around the prison. _____*past continuous*_____

12. Some prisoners were talking to Semevitch. _____

13. Aksenoff had been in prison for twenty-six years. _____

14. He has been very unhappy. _____

15. His children have forgotten him. _____

16. He has become old. _____

17. A guard had seen some earth on the road. _____

18. They have searched the prison. _____

19. The warden had spoken to Aksenoff. _____

20. Semevitch's heart was pounding with fear. _____

Exercise E

Combining sentences. Combine the two sentences into one. Write the sentence on the line. The first one has been done for you.

1. Aksenoff thought about his wife. He thought about his children.

   Aksenoff thought about his wife and children.

2. Aksenoff used to be young. He used to be happy.

   _____.

3. Aksenoff saw some earth. It was near one of the bunks.

   _____

   _____.

4. Semevitch had been digging a tunnel. It was under the wall.

   _____

   _____.

5. A guard noticed some earth. The earth was fresh.

   _____.

6. The warden spoke to Semevitch. The warden also spoke to Aksenoff.

   _____.

7. Aksenoff was an old man. He was truthful.

   _____.

8. Semevitch began to cry. Aksenoff began to cry too.

   _____.

Exercise F

Vocabulary review. Write a complete sentence for each word or group of words.

1. revenge _____

_____

2. glared _____

_____

3. confess _____

_____

4. trembled _____

_____

5. admitted _____

_____

6. release _____

_____

7. grief _____

_____

8. peered _____

_____

9. image _____

_____

10. bear in mind _____

_____

Sharing with Others

Everyone can learn by sharing ideas. Meet with your partner or group to discuss these questions. Write your answer to one of the questions.

◆ Aksenoff told Semevitch, "I have nothing to gain by escaping. And as for killing me, you killed me long ago." What did Aksenoff mean by these words?

◆ Many readers think that the story has a sad ending. Some readers, however, believe that the ending is a happy one. What do you think? Give reasons to support your answer.

_____

_____

_____

_____

_____

_____

_____

_____

_____

_____

_____

_____

_____

IRREGULAR VERBS

Verb	Past Tense	Past Participle
be (am/is/are)	was/were	been
become	became	become
begin	began	begun
bring	brought	brought
build	built	built
buy	bought	bought
catch	caught	caught
cut	cut	cut
come	came	come
die	died	died
do	did	done
drive	drove	driven
eat	ate	eaten
fall	fell	fallen
find	found	found
fly	flew	flown
get	got	gotten
give	gave	given
go	went	gone
grow	grew	grown
have	had	had
hear	heard	heard
hold	held	held

Verb	Past Tense	Past Participle
keep	kept	kept
know	knew	known
leave	left	left
lie	lay	lain
lose	lost	lost
make	made	made
put	put	put
ride	rode	ridden
run	ran	run
say	said	said
see	saw	seen
sell	sold	sold
send	sent	sent
set	set	set
shake	shook	shaken
sit	sat	sat
sleep	slept	slept
speak	spoke	spoken
spend	spent	spent
steal	stole	stolen
strike	struck	struck
take	took	taken
teach	taught	taught
tell	told	told
think	thought	thought
throw	threw	thrown

SCORE CHART

This is the Score Chart for YOU CAN ANSWER THESE QUESTIONS. Shade in your score for each part of the story. For example, if your score was 80 for Part 1 of **The Boy Who Drew Cats**, look at the bottom of the chart for Part 1, **The Boy Who Drew Cats**. Shade in the bar up to the 80 mark. By looking at this chart, you can see how well you did on each part of the story.

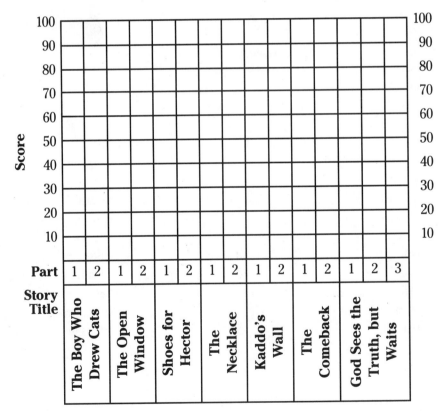

Score														
Part	1	2	1	2	1	2	1	2	1	2	1	2	1	2	3
Story Title	The Boy Who Drew Cats		The Open Window		Shoes for Hector		The Necklace		Kaddo's Wall		The Comeback		God Sees the Truth, but Waits		